Slow Cooker Recipes

An Easy and Healthy Cookbook to Make Your Life Easier

Jolene Keith

Copyright © 2017 by Jolene Keith - All rights reserved.

The follow eBook is reproduced below with the goal of providing information that is as accurate and reliable as possible. Regardless, purchasing this eBook can be seen as consent to the fact that both the publisher and the author of this book are in no way experts on the topics discussed within and that any recommendations or suggestions that are made herein are for entertainment purposes only. Professionals should be consulted as needed prior to undertaking any of the action endorsed herein.

This declaration is deemed fair and valid by both the American Bar Association and the Committee of Publishers Association and is legally binding throughout the United States.

Furthermore, the transmission, duplication or reproduction of any of the following work including specific information will be considered an illegal act irrespective of if it is done electronically or in print. This extends to creating a secondary or tertiary copy of the work or a recorded copy and is only allowed with express written consent from the Publisher. All additional right reserved.

The information in the following pages is broadly considered to be a truthful and accurate account of facts and as such any inattention, use or misuse of the information in question by the reader will render any resulting actions solely under their purview. There are no scenarios in which the publisher or the original author of this work can be in any fashion deemed liable for any hardship or damages that may befall them after undertaking information described herein.

Additionally, the information in the following pages is intended only for informational purposes and should thus be thought of as universal. As befitting its nature, it is presented without assurance regarding its prolonged validity or interim quality. Trademarks that are mentioned are done without written consent and can in no way be considered an endorsement from the trademark holder.

Table of Contents

Introduction 1

Chapter 1: Breakfast 3

    Bacon, Egg & Hash Brown Casserole 4

    Slow Cooker Apple Crisp 6

    Pumpkin French Toast 8

    Banana Bread Oatmeal 9

    Breakfast Potatoes 10

    Pumpkin Applesauce 11

    Breakfast Stuffed Peppers 13

    Kale, Feta, and Roasted Red Pepper Frittata 15

    Sausage Breakfast Casserole 17

    Peanut Butter Banana Slow Cooker Oatmeal 19

    Quinoa Energy Bar 20

    Blueberry Overnight French Toast 22

    Crust-Less Spinach Quiche 24

    Cream Slow Cooker Rice Pudding 26

    Breakfast Tater Tot Casserole 27

Chapter 2: Soups and Stews 29

    Honey Balsamic Beef Stew 30

    Butternut Squash Soup 32

    Irish Stew 34

Chicken Taco Soup 36

Turkey Barley Soup 38

Green Chili Enchilada Soup 39

French Onion Soup 41

Creamy Chicken and Gnocchi Soup 43

Potato Soup 45

White Chicken Chili 47

Chicken and Rice Soup 49

Root Vegetable Stew 51

Slow Cooker Shrimp, Chicken and Sausage Gumbo 52

Moroccan Lamb Stew 54

Cooker Chicken Noodle Soup 56

Chapter 3: Beans 58

Ham and White Beans 59

Kielbasas and BBQ Beans 60

Slow Cooker Pinto Beans 62

Red Beans and Rice 64

Ham and Bean Soup 66

Slow Cooker Black Bean Soup 68

Vegetarian Chili Mac 70

Green Bean Casserole 72

White Bean French Onion Soup 74

Cuban Black Beans 76

Barbecued Green Beans 78

Refried Black Beans 80

Bean and Potato Soup 82

Calico Beans... 84

Roasted Sweet Potato and Black Bean Chili 85

Chapter 4: Grains and Pastas 87

Four Cheese Mac n' Cheese 88

Chicken Parmesan and Pasta 90

Rustic Herbed Brown Rice 92

Pasta Fagioli Soup.. 93

Mushroom Risotto 95

Creamy Polenta.. 97

Spanish Rice.. 98

Beef Barley Soup 99

Buffalo Chicken Pasta 101

Cheesy Garlic Parmesan Spinach Orzo 103

Chicken and Mushroom Stroganoff................................... 104

Low-Carb Lasagna... 105

Cilantro Lime Rice 107

Three Cheese Jalapeno Bacon Mac n' Cheese................... 109

Mushroom and Wild Rice Pilaf 111

Chapter 5: Meat 112

Ultimate Slow Cooker Pot Roast 113

Brown Sugar Pineapple Ham... 115

Broccoli Beef 116

Pot Roast Chicken 118

Easy BBQ Ribs 120

Beef Tips and Gravy 121

Honey Pork Roast 123

Italian Beef Sandwiches 125

BBQ Beef Brisket 127

Mongolian Chicken 129

Chicken Cordon Bleu Casserole 130

Cubed Steak with Gravy 131

Slow Cooker Taco Meat 132

Cajun Chicken and Rice 133

Lentil Sloppy Joes 135

Chapter 6: Seafood **137**

Clam Chowder 138

BBQ Shrimp 140

Indian Fish Curry 141

Slow Cooker Salmon 143

Shrimp Scampi 144

New Orleans Spicy BBQ Shrimp 145

Maple Salmon 147

Salmon Curry 148

Lemon Dill Halibut 150

Red Curry with Cod 151

Coconut Cilantro Curry Shrimp 153

Cilantro Lime Fish Tacos 155

Shrimp and Cheese Grits 156

Fire Roasted Shrimp Tacos 157

Low Country Boil 158

Chapter 7: Vegetables 160

Cheddar Corn 161

Slow Cooker Mashed Potatoes 162

Garlic Parmesan Spaghetti Squash 163

Butternut Squash and Apples 164

Corn and Potato Chowder 165

Balsamic Brussels Sprouts 167

Onion Potatoes 169

Honey Cinnamon Carrots 170

Cabbage Roll Casserole 171

Easy Slow Cooker Veggies 172

Beef Vegetable Stew 173

Lentil and Vegetable Soup 175

Pumpkin Applesauce 177

Sweet Potato Casserole 178

Ratatouille Pasta 180

Chapter 8: Sauces 181

Homemade Slow Cooker Tomato Sauce (Made with FRESH Tomatoes!) 182

Meat Lover's Spaghetti Sauce 184

Slow Cooker Marinara 186

Bolognese Sauce 187

Short Rib Sauce 189

Chapter 9: Desserts and Sweets **191**

Caramel Apple Crumble 192

Caramel Peanut Butter Hot Fudge 194

Brownie Pudding 196

Caramel Cake 197

Cinnamon Roll Monkey Bread 198

Apple Dump Cake 199

Dulce De Leche 200

Caramel Blondies 201

Slow Cooker Candy 203

S'mores Brownies 204

Slow Cooker Chocolate Cake 206

Pumpkin Chocolate Lava Cake 208

Maple Pumpkin Spice Chex Mix 210

Pumpkin Pie Cake 212

Peach Cobbler 214

Conclusion **215**

Introduction

Congratulations on purchasing *Slow Cooker Recipes*. Thank you so much for doing so!

You probably stumbled across this book in the hunt for ways to make your fast-paced life more convenient. Well, I can tell you that you have come across an awesome resource that will assist you in fueling your body with delicious and satisfying meals in a short time with hardly any work.

This book was created for the folks in the world that love creating delicious eats from the comfort of their own kitchen, but do not have the time to spare. It's time to dust off that cooker that has been sitting in the back of the cabinet and put it to good use!

You will see as you skim this cookbook that there are a plethora of good eats for any time of the day that can be made right in the convenience of the cooker. Whether you are craving something to satisfy your sweet tooth, would rather have breakfast for dinner, or looking for something quick to whip up for a last-minute family get-together, this book will become your go-to resource for tasty meals and treats!

While there are truckloads of slow cooker books on the market, there are none quite like this one! It was written for people just like you, who are constantly hustling but still want to fuel their body with the best food possible. That being said, thanks again for choosing this particular cooker recipe book! Every effort was made to ensure it is full of as much useful information as possible, please enjoy and have fun skimming, finding, and creating your slow cooker recipes!

Chapter 1: Breakfast

Bacon, Egg & Hash Brown Casserole

What's in it:

- ¼ tsp. pepper
- ½ tsp. salt
- ½ C. milk
- 12 eggs
- 6 sliced green onions
- 8 ounces shredded cheddar cheese
- 8 slices heated/chopped bacon
- 20 ounces shredded hash browns

How it's made:

- Grease your cooker.
- Place hash browns in the base of cooker, sprinkle with half of bacon, a third of green onions, and half of the cheese. Set aside some of onions and bacon to garnish after heating, but place another layer of hash brown, bacon, and cheese.
- Whisk pepper, salt, and eggs together. Pour over top of components in cooker.
- Set to heat on high 2-3 hours or 4-5 hours on low.

- Sprinkle remaining onions and bacon. Serve with a few drops of hot sauce!

Slow Cooker Apple Crisp

What's in it:

Cinnamon Oat Crumble:

- 4 tbsp. melted coconut oil or butter
- Pinch of salt
- 1 tsp. cinnamon
- 1/3 C. brown sugar
- ½ C. all-purpose flour
- 2/3 C. sliced almonds
- 1 C. old-fashioned oats

Apple Crisp:

- Pinch of salt
- 2 tsp. cinnamon
- 1/3 C. brown sugar
- 1 tbsp. lemon juice
- 8 peeled/cored/slices apples of choice

How it's made:

- Toss lemon juice and apples together. Sprinkle with salt, cinnamon, and brown sugar. Pour into your cooker, ensuring to spread out evenly.
- To make the cinnamon oat crumble, combine all of crumble components together till combined. Toss with melted butter.
- Sprinkle apples in cooker with oat crumble.
- Set a few paper towels over cooker and cover with lid. This will produce condensation that will help to form that addicting crispy crumble!
- Set to heat on high 3-4 hours or low 6-8 hours. Apples should be tender and heated thoroughly.

Pumpkin French Toast

What's in it:

- 12 ounce whole-wheat bread, sliced into 1-2" cubes
- ¼ tsp. salt
- 2 tsp. vanilla extract
- 2 tsp. cinnamon
- 2 tsp. pumpkin pie spice
- 3 beaten eggs
- ½ C. coconut sugar
- 3 ½ C. milk
- 1 C. pumpkin puree

How it's made:

- Mix spices, eggs, coconut sugar, milk, and pumpkin puree together till incorporated.
- Place bread cubes in bowl and coat all well with pumpkin mixture. Cover and chill in the fridge to allow all that goodness to soak into the bread.
- Grease your cooker and add pumpkin mixture, spreading out evenly.
- Heat on low 7-8 hours.

Banana Bread Oatmeal

What's in it:

- 6 tbsp. raw walnuts, chopped
- ¼ C. pure maple syrup
- ½ tsp. nutmeg
- ½ tsp. salt
- 1 tsp. cinnamon
- 6 tbsp. flaxseed
- 3 mashed ripe bananas
- 1 C. steel-cut oats
- 4 C. unsweetened almond milk
- 3 C. water

How it's made:

- Pour nutmeg, salt, cinnamon, flaxseed, bananas, oats, 1 cup of almond milk and water into your cooker. Set to low and heat 6-8 hours till oats are soft but still chewy.
- Top with remaining almond milk, walnuts, and maple syrup.

Breakfast Potatoes

What's in it:

- Pepper and salt
- 2 tbsp. extra-virgin olive oil
- 2 tbsp. unsalted butter
- 2 tsp. smoked paprika
- 2 tsp. seasoned salt
- 3 minced cloves garlic
- ½ diced yellow onion
- 1 diced red bell pepper
- 1 diced green bell pepper
- 3 pounds baby potatoes, quartered

How it's made:

- Grease your cooker. Then pour in butter, paprika, seasoned salt, garlic, onion, bell peppers, and potatoes. Drizzle with olive oil and mix to incorporate.
- Heat on high 2 ½ - 3 hours or low 4-5 hours till potatoes are tender.
- Season with pepper and salt when serving!

Pumpkin Applesauce

What's in it:

- 5 scoops protein collagen peptides
- ½ C. water
- ½ tsp. nutmeg
- ½ tsp. ginger
- 1 tsp. pumpkin pie spice
- 1 ½ tsp. cinnamon
- 1 ½ tsp. pure vanilla extract
- 3 tbsp. pure maple syrup
- 15 ounces pumpkin puree
- 8 green apples

Optional toppings:

- Coconut flakes
- Chopped pecans
- Chopped walnuts

How it's made:

- Peel and cut apples into cubes. Pour into cooker. Then top apples with remaining recipe ingredients.
- Set to heat on low 4-6 hours till apples become heated and tenderized and can be mashed with ease.
- If you desire chunkier applesauce, mash with large spoon. For smoother applesauce, pour mixture into a food processor and blend till you achieve your desired consistency.
- Enjoy as is or mix in some of your favorite yogurt!

Breakfast Stuffed Peppers

What's in it:

- 1/8 tsp. pepper
- ¼ tsp. salt
- 4 ounces fire-roasted green chilies, chopped
- 4 ounces marble jack cheese
- 6 eggs
- 4 bell peppers of your choice of color
- ½ pound ground breakfast sausage

How it's made:

- Brown sausage till heated and then drain grease.
- Pour half a cup of water into the base of your cooker.
- Wash peppers and cut off tops. Then clean out middles and place peppers into your cooker.
- Combine eggs, green chilies, and shredded cheese. Season with pepper and salt. Spoon cheese filling into peppers in the cooker.
- Set to heat on high 2-3 hours or set to low to heat 4-6 hours till eggs are heated.

- Sprinkle with cilantro and green onion when serving.

Kale, Feta, and Roasted Red Pepper Frittata

What's in it:

- ½ tsp. all-purpose seasoning blend
- 8 beaten eggs
- 4-5 ounces crumbled feta cheese
- ¼ C. green onion
- 6 ounces diced roasted red pepper
- 5 ounces baby kale
- 1-2 tsp. olive oil
- Pepper
- Low-fat sour cream

How it's made:

- Wash kale and dry with paper towels.
- Warm up oil and sauté 3-4 minutes till softened.
- Drain and chop up peppers. Crumble feta and slice green onions. Place onion, red peppers, and kale into the cooker. Beat eggs and pour over other components in cooker. Stir to combine. Season with pepper and sprinkle feta cheese over.

- Set to heat on low 2-3 hours till cheese is melted and frittata is set.
- Serve with a dollop of sour cream.

Sausage Breakfast Casserole

What's in it:

- ¼ tsp. pepper
- ½ tsp. salt
- ½ C. milk
- 12 eggs
- 6 sliced green onions
- ½ C. sun-dried tomatoes
- ½ C. shredded parmesan cheese
- 2 C. shredded mozzarella cheese
- 1 package sausage crumbles
- 1 package frozen hash browns

How it's made:

- Grease cooker. Split hash browns in half and pout half into the base of your cooker.
- Pour half of green onion, half of tomatoes, half of both cheeses, and half the sausage over layer of hash browns.
- Repeat the last step by layering remaining ingredients.

- Beat pepper, salt, milk, and eggs together and pour over casserole layers.
- Set to heat on low 8 hours or set to heat on high 4 hours till eggs are set.

Peanut Butter Banana Slow Cooker Oatmeal

What's in it:

- 1 tbsp. chia seeds
- 1 tsp. vanilla extract
- 1 tsp. cinnamon
- ¼ C. peanut or almond butter
- 3 C. unsweetened vanilla almond milk
- 1 C. steel cut oats
- 2 mashed ripe bananas

How it's made:

- Combine all recipe components together till incorporated. Pour mixture into cooker and pour in a cup of water.
- Set to heat on low 6-8 hours, making sure to occasionally stir. Enjoy!

Quinoa Energy Bar

What's in it:

- 2 tbsp. chia seeds
- 1/3 C. chopped dried apples
- 1/3 C. chopped roasted almond
- ½ C. raisins
- 1/3 C. unheated quinoa
- 2 eggs
- ½ tsp. cinnamon
- Pinch of salt
- 1 C. unsweetened vanilla almond milk
- 2 tbsp. pure maple syrup
- 2 tbsp. almond butter

How it's made:

- Grease your cooker.
- Melt maple syrup and almond butter together for 30 seconds till butter is creamy.
- Whisk syrup and mix in salt, cinnamon, and almond milk till incorporated.

- Whisk eggs and then stir in with cinnamon mixture. Mix in all remaining recipe components till combined.
- Add mixture to cooker. Set to heat on low 3 ½ - 4 hours.
- Run butter knife round the outside of heated mixture. Then pop in the fridge to cool. When cooled, cut into bars and enjoy!

Blueberry Overnight French Toast

What's in it:

- ½ tsp. salt
- 1 tsp. vanilla extract
- 1 ½ C. while milk
- 1 ½ C. frozen blueberries
- 5 beaten eggs
- 12 slices whole wheat or whole-grain bread
- ¼ C. melted butter
- 1 ¼ tsp. cinnamon
- 1 C. brown sugar

Garnish Options:

- Fresh blueberries
- Whipped cream
- Maple syrup

How it's made:

- Mix butter, cinnamon, and brown sugar together. Sprinkle a third of mixture into the base of a greased cooker.

- Cover mixture with six slices of bread. Top with 1/3 of cinnamon mixture. Scatter berries, sprinkle with remaining bread and top with remaining cinnamon mixture.
- Beat salt, vanilla extract, milk, and eggs together. Add to the cooker and press down gently with a large spoon. Cover and place in fridge to chill overnight.
- The next day, set cooker to heat on low 3-4 hours till mixture is lightly browned and eggs are set.
- Serve with fresh blueberries, a dollop of whipped cream and maple syrup.

Crust-Less Spinach Quiche

What's in it:

- ¼ tsp. baking soda
- ½ C. ground almond flour
- ¼ tsp. pepper
- ½ tsp. salt
- 2 tbsp. chives
- 1 C. sour cream
- 8 eggs
- 1 ½ C. shredded cheddar cheese
- 1 red bell pepper
- 2 C. baby bella mushrooms
- 1 tbsp. ghee
- 10 ounces frozen spinach

How it's made:

- With butter, grease your cooker.
- Squeeze water from spinach and lay out on paper towels to drain.

- Warm up a tbsp of ghee and sauté mushrooms and peppers for 4 minutes till fragrant.
- Mix pepper, salt, sour cream, and eggs together. Mix in chives and shredded cheese till incorporated.
- Combine baking soda and almond flour in a bowl and fold in egg mixture.
- Add veggies to egg mixture and place into cooker.
- Set to heat on high 2 ½ hours or set to heat on low 4-5 hours.

Cream Slow Cooker Rice Pudding

What's in it:

- 2 tbsp. butter
- 1 tsp. vanilla extract
- 1 tsp. cinnamon
- ½ C. sugar
- 4 C. milk
- ¾ C. long-grain white rice

How it's made:

- Rinse rice in cold water.
- Pour all ingredients into cooker and mix in sugar till it dissolves. Incorporate all components well.
- Set to heat on high 2 ½ - 3 hours till rice is creamy.

Breakfast Tater Tot Casserole

What's in it:

- 1 C. shredded Colby jack cheese
- 1/8 tsp. pepper
- ¼ tsp. salt
- ½ tsp. garlic powder
- ½ tsp. thyme
- 2 tbsp. heavy cream
- 6 eggs
- 1 pound ground turkey sausage
- 32 ounces frozen tater tots

How it's made:

- Grease cooker.
- Add 2/3 of tater tots to the base of cooker.
- Stir pepper, salt, garlic powder, thyme, cream, and eggs together. Then pour over tater tots in cooker.
- Brown sausage till heated. Then pour into cooker.
- Top with remaining tater tots and Colby jack cheese.

- Set to heat on high 2-3 hours or set to heat on low 4-6 hours.

Chapter 2: Soups and Stews

Honey Balsamic Beef Stew

What's in it:

- 2 tbsp. cornstarch
- ¼ tsp. pepper
- 1 tsp. seasoning salt
- 2 tsp. minced garlic
- 1 tbsp. Worcestershire sauce
- 2 tbsp. tomato paste
- 1/3 C. liquid honey
- 1/3 C. balsamic vinegar
- ¼ C. low-sodium beef broth
- ½ chopped onion
- 2 peeled/chopped carrots
- 1 chopped stalk celery
- 1 pound stewing beef
- 1 pound little potatoes

How it's made:

- Pour onions, carrots, celery, beef, and potatoes into a cooker.

- Mix pepper, salt, cornstarch, garlic, Worcestershire sauce, tomato paste, honey, vinegar, and broth together. Pour into cooker.
- Set to heat on low 8 hours till carrots and potatoes become softened.

Butternut Squash Soup

What's in it:

- ½ C. unsweetened coconut milk
- Pinch of nutmeg
- Pinch of cinnamon
- 1/8 tsp. cayenne pepper
- ¼ tsp. pepper
- ½ tsp. salt
- 1 diced onion
- 1 sprig sage
- 1 butternut squash
- 1 granny smith apple
- 1 carrot
- 2 cloves minced/peeled garlic
- 2 C. vegetable stock

How it's made:

- Cut up squash, carrots, and apple.

    Pour vegetable stock into cooker along with nutmeg, cinnamon, cayenne, pepper, salt, onion, sage, butternut squash, apple, carrot, and garlic.

- Set to heat on low 6-8 hours or set to heat on high 3-4 hours. Squash should be tender.
- Remove sage and stir in coconut milk.
- With an immersion blender, puree soup till its smooth. Season with cayenne, pepper, and salt if needed to achieve desired taste.

Irish Stew

What's in it:

- 4 ounces stout beer
- ¼ C. flour
- 1 ½ C. beef broth
- 3 ounces tomato paste
- ½ tsp. salt
- 2 tsp. steak seasoning blend
- 1 clove of garlic
- ½ white onion
- ½ pound baby carrots
- 1 pound white baby potatoes
- 1 ½ pounds boneless pork shoulder

How it's made:

- Cut up potatoes and pork into bite sized chunks and pour into cooker along with carrots.
- Peel and dice garlic and onion and place into cooker.
- Sprinkle with seasonings and pour in beef broth.

- Whisk flour and water together till a smooth paste is created and dump into cooker.
- Stir to incorporate. Then pour in beer.
- Set to heat on low 8 hours.

Chicken Taco Soup

What's in it:

- 1 pound boneless skinless chicken breasts
- 2 C. low-sodium chicken broth
- 3 tbsp. taco seasoning
- 14.5 ounces diced tomatoes
- 15 ounces corn
- 1 can pinto beans
- 1 can black beans
- 1 C. mild salsa

Optional Toppings:

- Tortilla chips
- Green onion
- Avocado
- Grated/shredded cheese
- Sour cream
- Greek yogurt
- Cilantro

How it's made:

- Pour chicken broth, taco seasoning, diced tomatoes, corn, salsa, pinto and black beans into cooker. Incorporate well.
- Place chicken into cooker so that all of liquid adequately covers meat.
- Set to heat on low 6 hours.
- Take out chicken. Shred or cut into bite sized chunks. Then incorporate chicken back into soup.
- Serve soup with desired toppings. Enjoy!

Turkey Barley Soup

What's in it:

- 12 C. turkey stock
- 1 C. rinsed barley
- 2 C. heated shredded turkey
- ¼ C. chopped parsley
- 2 C. chopped carrots
- 2 C. sliced celery
- 1 chopped yellow onion

How it's made:

- Combine turkey stock, barley, turkey, parsley, carrots, celery, and onion within your cooker.
- Set to heat on low 6-7 hours or set to heat on high 4 hours.
- Serve while hot and sprinkle with additional parsley.

Green Chili Enchilada Soup

What's in it:

- Pepper and salt
- 8 ounces softened cream cheese
- 1 tsp. garlic powder
- 1 tsp. onion powder
- 1 tbsp. chili powder
- 2 tbsp. cumin
- ¾ C. water
- 4 ounces diced green chilies
- 15 ounces salsa
- 24 ounces boneless chicken thighs or breasts
- 32 ounces chicken broth

Optional Garnishes:

- Sour cream
- Avocado
- Shredded cheese

How it's made:

- Put chicken into the base of your cooker.
- Mix chili powder, garlic powder, cumin, onion powder, cumin, water, green chilies, salsa, and broth together and then pour over chicken.
- Set to heat on low 7 hours.
- Take out chicken and shred with forks. Dump back into cooker.
- Add cream cheese and heat half an hour more.
- Top with desired garnishes when serving.

French Onion Soup

What's in it:

- 6 tbsp. parmesan cheese
- ½ C. shredded emmental cheese
- ¾ C. shredded Gruyere cheese
- 8 slices French bread
- 1 bay leaf
- 4 sprigs thyme
- 1/3 C. dry sherry
- 1 minced clove garlic
- 1 tbsp. Worcestershire sauce
- 64 ounces beef broth
- 2 tbsp. brown sugar
- 3 tbsp. butter
- 3 sliced white onions

How it's made:

- Heat onions with brown sugar and butter in a pan 20 minutes till caramelized.

- Once gold, pour into you cooker and pour in remaining recipe components, minus the cheeses.

- Set to heat on low 6-8 hours.

- Take out and discard bay leaf. Spoon mixture into bowls. Top with bread slices and cheese.

- Broil 2-3 minutes till cheese melts and bread becomes a bit crisped.

Creamy Chicken and Gnocchi Soup

What's in it:

- Pepper and salt
- 2 C. baby spinach
- 2/3 C. half and half
- 1 ½ tbsp. flour
- 32 ounces chicken broth
- ¾ - 1 pound chopped rotisserie chicken
- 1 package gnocchi
- ¼ chopped yellow onion
- 3 chopped cloves garlic
- 3 tbsp. butter

How it's made:

- Melt butter and sauté onion and garlic together for 60 seconds till fragrant. Then pour in chicken, broth, and gnocchi. Heat mixture to boiling point and heat 3 minutes till gnocchi is tenderized.
- Mix in half and half and flour. Stir till mixture comes up to boiling point again.

- Remove from heat and add in spinach leave. With pepper and salt, season to reach desired taste. Serve!

Potato Soup

What's in it:

- ½ tsp. pepper
- 1 tsp. salt
- ½ C. Greek yogurt
- 1 C. shredded sharp cheddar cheese
- 12 ounces evaporated milk
- 1/3 C. all-purpose flour
- 3 tbsp. bacon grease
- 1 diced onion
- 2 pounds Yukon potatoes
- 3-4 C. chicken stock
- 6 slices heated/diced bacon

How it's made:

- Place onion, potatoes, 3 cups of chicken stock, and bacon to your cooker. Combine well. Set to heat on low 6-8 hours or set to heat on low 3-4 hours till potatoes become tender.
- Once soup is ready to eat, melt butter and mix in flour, stirring 1 minute. Gradually pour in

evaporated milk till mixture becomes smooth. Bring to a simmer and let it heat till very thickened.

- Pour milk mixture into the cooker. Then mix in yogurt, cheese, pepper, and salt.
- For thicker soup, mash potatoes a bit. If you like thinner soup, add 1-2 cups of warmed stock. Use pepper and salt to reach desired taste.
- Serve with toppings of choice.

White Chicken Chili

What's in it:

- ½ C. chopped cilantro
- Juice of ½ lime
- 14 ounces full-fat coconut milk
- 4 C. chicken broth
- ¼ tsp. pepper
- 1 tsp. salt
- 2 tsp. chili powder
- 1 tsp. oregano
- 2 ½ tsp. cumin
- 6 minced cloves garlic
- 1 diced jalapeno pepper
- 1 bell pepper
- 1 diced onion
- 1 tbsp. avocado oil
- 1 ½ pounds boneless skinless chicken breasts

How it's made:

- Place spices, garlic, peppers, and onions into the base of your cooker. Put chicken over the top of veggies in a single and even layer.

- Pour chicken broth over veggies and chicken.

- Set to heat on low 7-8 hours till chicken is heated thoroughly and veggies become nice and tender.

- Take out chicken and shred and then dump back in cooker. Set to heat on high. Pour in coconut milk and heat 10-15 minutes till soup is heated thoroughly.

- Mix in cilantro and lime juice. Taste and season to achieve your desired flavor. Serve with lime wedges and cilantro.

Chicken and Rice Soup

What's in it:

- 9 C. chicken broth
- 2 tbsp. butter
- 1 bay leaf
- ½ tsp. sage
- ½ tsp. rosemary
- 2 tsp. parsley
- 3 tsp. salt
- Pepper
- 3 minced cloves garlic
- 3 chopped celery stalks
- 3 chopped carrots
- 1 chopped onion
- 1 C. brown rice
- 3 chicken breasts (cut in half and trimmed of fat)

How it's made:

- Pour all recipe components into your cooker, minus the rice.
- Set to heat on low for 4 hours. Add rice halfway through the heating cycle.
- Half an hour before preparing to serve, take out chicken and shred. Place chicken back into slow heat and heat 30 minutes.

Root Vegetable Stew

What's in it:

- ½ tsp. salt
- 1 tsp. ginger
- 1 minced clove garlic
- ¼ C. coconut aminos
- ¼ C. apple cider vinegar
- 1 chopped sweet potato
- 1 chopped onion
- ½ pound chopped parsnips
- ½ pound chopped carrots
- 1 pound chopped beef

How it's made:

- Pour all recipe components into a cooker and stir to thoroughly incorporate.
- Set cooker to heat on high 3 hours. Enjoy!

Slow Cooker Shrimp, Chicken and Sausage Gumbo

What's in it:

- 1 1/3 C. heated rice
- 1 tsp. oregano
- 1 tsp. thyme
- 1 tbsp. Cajun spice
- 2 C. chicken broth
- 3 tsp. minced garlic
- 28 ounces diced tomatoes
- 3 diced celery ribs
- 1 hot pepper of choice (habanera, scotch bonnet, Serrano, jalapeno, etc)
- 1 diced green pepper
- 1 diced onion
- 1 pound raw/shelled shrimp
- 1 pound smoked sausage of choice (garlic sausage, farmer's sausage, kielbasa, etc.)
- 1 pound chicken breast

How it's made:

- Place all recipe components into a cooker minus rice and shrimp.
- Set to heat on low 6-7 hours, ensuring to stir on occasion.
- In the last hour of cooking, lightly salt shrimp and pour into cooker. During the last 30 minutes, add rice and combine. Heat till rice is heated through.
- Serve with crusty bread. Enjoy!

Moroccan Lamb Stew

What's in it:

- 15 ounces chickpeas
- 2 ½ C. beef broth
- 6 halved plum tomatoes
- ½ tsp. ginger
- 1 tsp. Moroccan spice blend
- 1 ½ tsp. allspice
- 1 bay leaf
- 1 cinnamon
- ½ C. dried apricots
- 3 chopped garlic coves
- 2 ½ pounds boneless leg of lamb
- 6 peeled/cubed Yukon potatoes
- 3 cubed carrots
- 1 chopped yellow onion
- Olive oil

How it's made:

- In a Dutch over, warm up 2 tbsp. olive oil and sauté potatoes, carrots, and onions for 4-5 minutes. Then season with pepper, salt, and garlic. Set to the side.
- Brown lamb while seasoning with pepper and salt. Place sautéed veggies back to pot with lamb. Then pour in bay leaf, spices, cinnamon, and dried apricots, coating well. Add tomatoes and broth and heat to boiling. Heat 5 minutes.
- Pour all components into a cooker and set to heat on high 3 ½ hours.
- Serve with pita bread, couscous, or rice. Devour!

Cooker Chicken Noodle Soup

What's in it:

- 1 tbsp. lemon juice
- ¼ C. chopped parsley
- 2 C. unheated egg noodles
- Pepper and salt
- 2 bay leaves
- ¼ tsp. crushed celery seed
- ½ tsp. sage
- ½ tsp. rosemary
- ¾ tsp. thyme
- 1 C. water
- 6 C. chicken broth
- 3 tbsp. extra-virgin olive oil
- 3-5 minced cloves garlic
- 4 stalks chopped celery
- 1 chopped yellow onion
- 5 chopped carrots
- 1 ½ pounds boneless skinless chicken thighs or breasts

How it's made:

- Place garlic, celery, onion, carrots, and chicken into cooker. Then add bay leaves, celery seeds, rosemary, thyme, water, broth, and olive oil. Season with pepper and salt.
- Set to heat on low 6-7 hours.
- Take out chicken and let sit 10 minutes. Cut chicken into bite sizes. Place parsley and egg noodles into cooker and heat 10 more minutes.
- Mix in lemon juice and return chicken to cooker. Stir to combine.
- Serve topped with parmesan cheese and with saltine crackers.

Chapter 3: Beans

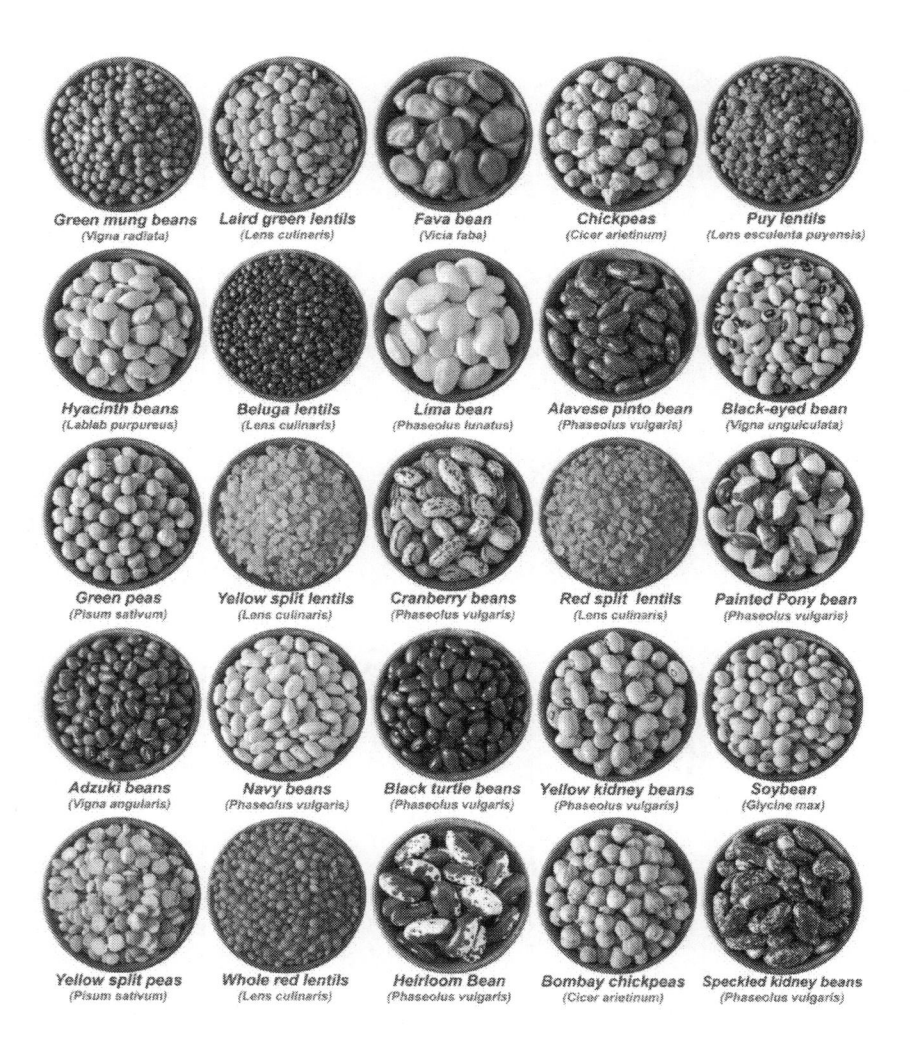

Green mung beans *(Vigna radiata)*	Laird green lentils *(Lens culinaris)*	Fava bean *(Vicia faba)*	Chickpeas *(Cicer arietinum)*	Puy lentils *(Lens esculenta puyensis)*
Hyacinth beans *(Lablab purpureus)*	Beluga lentils *(Lens culinaris)*	Lima bean *(Phaseolus lunatus)*	Alavese pinto bean *(Phaseolus vulgaris)*	Black-eyed bean *(Vigna unguiculata)*
Green peas *(Pisum sativum)*	Yellow split lentils *(Lens culinaris)*	Cranberry beans *(Phaseolus vulgaris)*	Red split lentils *(Lens culinaris)*	Painted Pony bean *(Phaseolus vulgaris)*
Adzuki beans *(Vigna angularis)*	Navy beans *(Phaseolus vulgaris)*	Black turtle beans *(Phaseolus vulgaris)*	Yellow kidney beans *(Phaseolus vulgaris)*	Soybean *(Glycine max)*
Yellow split peas *(Pisum sativum)*	Whole red lentils *(Lens culinaris)*	Heirloom Bean *(Phaseolus vulgaris)*	Bombay chickpeas *(Cicer arietinum)*	Speckled kidney beans *(Phaseolus vulgaris)*

Ham and White Beans

What's in it:

- Pepper and salt
- 6 C. water
- 2 tsp. onion powder
- 1 pound diced ham, shanks, hocks, or ham bone
- 1 pounds package dried northern beans

How it's made:

- Sort beans to ensure there are no pebbles. Rinse beans.
- Add choice of ham, pepper, salt, onion powder, and rinsed beans to cooker.
- Set to heat on low 8 hours till beans become tender.
- If using hocks, shanks, or ham bone, remove bone and take off meat. Shred and return meat to cooker. Heat till warmed through.
- Serve with cornbread and enjoy!

Kielbasas and BBQ Beans

What's in it:

- 2 pounds kielbasa (cut into pieces)
- ½ pound bacon, heated/cut into pieces
- 14 ½ ounces chicken broth
- ½ C. maple syrup
- 1 tbsp. apple cider vinegar
- 1 tsp. chili powder
- 1 tbsp. mustard
- 1 tbsp. Worcestershire sauce
- ¾ C. ketchup
- ½ BBQ sauce
- 1 diced onion
- 1 can kidney beans
- 2 cans great northern beans
- 2 cans black beans

How it's made:

- Drain and rinse all beans. Pour all recipe components into cooker and stir well to incorporate.
- Place kielbasa over the top.
- Set to heat on low 6-8 hours or set to heat on high 4-5 hours. Make sure to stir well to incorporate all ingredients before dishing up and enjoying!

Slow Cooker Pinto Beans

What's in it:

- 1 tsp. pepper
- 1 tsp. onion powder
- 1 tsp. garlic powder
- 1 onion
- 2-3 ham hocks
- 2 C. water
- 6 C. chicken broth
- 20 ounce bag pinto beans with ham flavor packet

How it's made:

- Pour water, broth, and beans without packet of seasoning into cooker. Mix well to combine. Place pieces of onion and ham hocks into liquid.
- Set to heat on high for 4 hours. Set the seasoning packet to the side.
- Add remaining spices and seasoning packet to the cooker, stir well and heat 2-4 more hours till beans are extremely tenderized.
- Take out ham hocks and onion pieces.

- Spoon out 2-3 cups of mixture and mash till smooth. Pour mashed beans back into cooker and combine. Leave beans uncovered for 60 minutes to rest.
- Cut meat off ham hocks and shred. Stir into bean mixture.
- Serve with heated onions and cornbread. Devour!

Red Beans and Rice

What's in it:

- 4 C. unheated long-grain rice
- 7 C. water
- ¼ tsp. chili powder
- ½ tsp. salt
- 1 tbsp. Worcestershire sauce
- 2 minced cloves of garlic
- 1 chopped onion
- 1 chopped green bell pepper
- 3 chopped celery ribs
- ½ pound sliced smoked sausage
- 1 pound rinsed dried red beans

Garnish:

- Parsley
- Green onions

How it's made:

- Add all recipe components to a cooker, minus rice.
- Set to heat on high 6 hours.
- Prepare rice by what the package instructions say.
- Plate red beans over the top of a serving of rice. Garnish with parsley and green onions.

Ham and Bean Soup

What's in it:

- 1 juiced lemon
- 15 ounce can diced tomatoes
- 1 tsp. chili powder
- 1 minced clove garlic
- 1 diced onion
- 1 ham bone with meat or 1 pound heated sausage
- 8 C. chicken broth
- 1 package Ham beans bean soup

Optional:

- Crushed red pepper
- Hot sauce

How it's made:

- Rinse and drain beans. Sort for unwanted debris and place seasoning packet to the side.
- Pour chili powder, garlic, broth, water, ham bone, onions, and beans into the cooker.
- Set to heat on high 5 hours till beans are tenderized.

- Take out ham bone and cut off meat. Add meat back into cooker. Mix in lemon juice, ham flavor packet, and diced tomatoes. Heat for another half an hour.

Slow Cooker Black Bean Soup

What's in it:

- 4 C. vegetable broth
- 2 bay leaves
- 1 tbsp. Worcestershire sauce
- 3 tsp. chipotle chili powder
- 3 tsp. cumin
- 2 tsp. oregano
- 3 minced cloves garlic
- 1 diced yellow onion
- 2 diced jalapeno pepper
- 1 diced bell pepper
- 1 can crushed fire-roasted tomatoes
- 2 C. dried black beans (soaked overnight and then rinsed)

How it's made:

- Pour all recipe components into your cooker. Set to heat on high 8 hours.
- Take out bay leaves when heating is complete.

- Scoop out several cups of soup and with an immersion blender, mix till pureed. Add pureed mixture back into slow heat and combine well.
- Serve nice and warm, topped with green onions, cilantro, and avocado.

Vegetarian Chili Mac

What's in it:

- 8 ounces whole-wheat unheated elbow macaroni pasta
- 1 ½ C. shredded cheddar cheese
- 2 C. vegetable broth
- 1/8 tsp. pepper
- ½ tsp. salt
- 2 tsp. cumin
- 1 ½ tbsp. chili powder
- 28 ounce can crushed tomatoes
- 15 ounces can kidney beans
- 15 ounce can pinto beans
- 1 chopped red bell pepper
- 1 chopped onion

How it's made:

- Pour all recipe components into cooker minus green onions, cheese, and pasta. Mix to combine thoroughly.
- Set to heat on high 4 hours or set to heat on low 6-8 hours.
- Mix in pasta and heat on high 20 minutes till pasta is heated through. Then stir in a cup of cheese.
- Serve topped with green onions and remaining shredded cheese. Enjoy!

Green Bean Casserole

What's in it:

- Pepper and salt
- 1 can fried onions
- 1 tsp. Worcestershire sauce
- ¼ C. flour
- 1 tsp. minced garlic
- ½ C. heavy cream
- ½ C. vegetable stock
- 1 can condensed cream of mushroom soup
- 3 can green beans

How it's made:

- Mix together all recipe components within the cooker, minus onions and green beans. Incorporate well.
- Add half of fried onions and green beans, stir well.
- Top with remaining onions and set to heat on high for 2 – 2 ½ hours.
- If you want a crisper casserole, top with onions towards the end of heating. You can also brown

onions on oven for a bit before pouring on the top of mixture for extra crunch!

White Bean French Onion Soup

What's in it:

- 6 C. vegetable stock
- 2 tsp. thyme leaves
- ½ tsp. pepper
- 1 tsp. oregano
- 2 cans white beans
- ¼ C. melted butter
- ½ tsp. salt
- 3 diced onions

Garnish:

- Shredded parmesan cheese
- Croutons

How it's made:

- Add melted butter, salt, and onions into your cooker. Combine and let onions caramelize for 3-5 hours within cooker.

- Pour in vegetable stock, thyme, pepper, oregano, and beans to cooker. Set to heat on high 3 hours.

- Garnish with parmesan cheese and croutons when serving!

Cuban Black Beans

What's in it:

- 1 chopped bunch of cilantro
- 2 juiced limes
- 6 C. water
- 1 pound dried black beans
- 2 tsp. salt
- 1 tsp. smoked paprika
- 1 bay leaf
- 1 tsp. cumin
- 1 chopped red bell pepper
- 1 diced jalapeno pepper
- 1 C. chopped red onion
- 2 tbsp. olive oil

How it's made:

- Sauté bell pepper, jalapeno, and red onion together for 3-5 minutes till softened in your cooker.

- Then add water, black beans, salt, bay leaf, paprika, bay leaf, cumin, and garlic to cooker. Set to heat on high 4 hours.
- Once heated, stir in cilantro and lime juice and devour.

Barbecued Green Beans

What's in it:

- 4 cans green beans
- ¼ tsp. cayenne pepper
- ¼ tsp. pepper
- ¼ tsp. salt
- 1 tbsp. Worcestershire sauce
- ¼ C. BBQ sauce
- 1/3 C. light brown sugar
- ½ C. ketchup
- ½ C. chopped onion
- 8 slices thick cut bacon

How it's made:

- Heat bacon till crispy and set to the side. Reserve 2 tbsp. of bacon grease and throw away the rest. Place onion into bacon grease that you reserved and heat till soft.
- Stir cayenne pepper, pepper, salt, Worcestershire sauce, BBQ sauce, brown sugar, and ketchup together.

- Grease your cooker and then add green beans. Pour onions and bacon grease over beans. Then mix in ketchup mixture into beans and combine well.
- Top with bacon. Set cooker to heat on low 4-5 hours.

Refried Black Beans

What's in it:

- ¼ C. butter
- 5 C. water
- 2 whole garlic cloves
- 4 chicken bouillon cubes
- ¼ tsp. pepper
- 1/8 tsp. cayenne pepper
- 1 slices white onion
- 1 pound black beans (soaked overnight)

How it's made:

- Soak black beans overnight. Drain beans and pour into your cooker.
- Warm up oil and brown slices of onion on both sides till toasted. Then pour onions into cooker.
- Pour water, chicken bouillon cubes, garlic cloves, pepper, and cayenne pepper into cooker. Set to heat on low 9 hours.

- Once heated, take out half of the heating juices. Pour beans into a blender and pulse till creamy. Season with pepper and salt to achieve desired taste.

Bean and Potato Soup

What's in it:

- 1 parmesan rind
- 1 tsp. crushed red pepper flakes
- ¼ tsp. pepper
- 1 tsp. salt
- 2 tbsp. thyme
- ½ tbsp. chopped oregano
- 2 tbsp. chopped rosemary
- ½ C. chopped celery
- ½ C. chopped carrots
- 2 minced garlic cloves
- ½ C. chopped onions
- 2 cans northern beans
- 1 pound peeled/chopped Yukon potatoes

How it's made:

- Pour all recipe components into your cooker. Mix well to ensure adequate incorporation.
- Set to heat on low 6-8 hours or set to heat on high 5 hours.
- Take out parmesan rind before serving. Enjoy!

Calico Beans

What's in it:

- 1 tsp. salt
- 1 tsp. mustard
- 1 tbsp. apple cider vinegar
- ½ C. ketchup
- ½ C. brown sugar
- 1 can lima beans
- 1 can kidney beans
- 1 can molasses beans and pork
- ½ C. chopped onion
- 1 pound lean ground beef
- 4 diced slices of thick cut bacon

How it's made:

- Heat back for 2-3 minutes and then add onion and beef, heating till meat has no visible pink areas. Drain grease.

- Pour meat mixture into cooker along with salt, mustard, ketchup, brown sugar, and beans. Set to heat on low 6-8 hours or set to heat on high 3-4 hours.

Roasted Sweet Potato and Black Bean Chili

What's in it:

- 2 can black beans
- 2 tsp. cinnamon
- 1 ½ tbsp. ancho chili powder
- 1 ear corn
- 2 cans fire-roasted diced tomatoes
- 2 ½ C. vegetable broth
- 4 minced cloves of garlic
- 1 diced red bell pepper
- 1 chopped yellow onion
- 2 tbsp. olive oil
- Pepper and salt
- 2 pounds sweet potatoes

Toppings:

- Mexican blended cheese
- Cheddar cheese
- Sour cream

- Roasted sliced jalapenos
- Diced avocado
- Lime wedges
- Cilantro

How it's made:

- Cut up potatoes into cubes, husk and cut kernels from corn, and rinse/drain black beans.
- Pour all recipe components into a cooker.
- Set to heat on high 5-6 hours or set to heat on low 7-9 hours.
- When done, serve up with desired toppings.

Chapter 4: Grains and Pastas

Four Cheese Mac n' Cheese

What's in it:

- 2 tbsp. chopped chives
- Pepper and salt
- ½ tsp. onion powder
- ½ tsp. paprika
- 2 tsp. Dijon mustard
- 1 can evaporated milk
- 3 C. whole milk
- ½ C. parmesan cheese
- 4 ounces cubed cream cheese
- 2 C. grated American cheese
- 2 C. shredded sharp cheddar cheese
- 1 pound elbow macaroni

How it's made:

- Pour parmesan cheese, cream cheese, American cheese, 1 cup of cheddar cheese, and macaroni into your cooker.

- Then stir in onion powder, paprika, Dijon mustard, evaporated milk, and milk, combining well. Season with pepper and salt to achieve desired taste.
- Set to heat on low 2 ½ hours till noodles are cooked and mixture is nice and creamy. Stir in remaining cheddar cheese and heat 2-4 minutes till melted. If you find the mixture to be too thick, add a bit more milk.
- Eat topped with chives. Enjoy!

Chicken Parmesan and Pasta

What's in it:

- ¼ C. parmesan cheese
- 3 C. mozzarella cheese
- 1 pound penne pasta
- ½ tsp. oregano
- ¼ tsp. pepper
- ¼ tsp. salt
- 1 ½ pounds boneless skinless chicken breasts
- 2 jars chunky tomatoes, onion and garlic sauce

How it's made:

- Place chicken into cooker. Season with oregano, pepper, and salt. Pour tomato sauce over chicken.
- Set to heat on high 4 hours or set to heat on low 6-8 hours.
- Once chicken is done, prepare pasta according to package directions. As pasta heats, take chicken out of cooker and cut into bite sized pieces. Pour chicken back into cooker.

- Drain pasta and pour into cooker. Stir in along with parmesan cheese and shredded mozzarella cheese. Heat 15 minutes on high till bubbly and cheese is melted.

Rustic Herbed Brown Rice

What's in it:

- Pepper and salt
- ½ tsp. oregano
- ½ tsp. thyme
- 4 C. beef broth
- 8 ounces sliced mushrooms
- 2 tbsp. butter
- 2 C. long grain brown rice
- Parsley, to garnish

How it's made:

- Melt butter and sauté rice for 2-4 minutes till just toasted. Pour rice into your cooker along with oregano, thyme, broth, and mushrooms. Pour in beef broth and mix well to ensure adequate incorporation.
- Set to heat on high 2-3 hours. Season with pepper and salt and garnish with parsley when serving.

Pasta Fagioli Soup

What's in it:

- 1 C. unheated pasta
- 1 can kidney beans
- 1 can cannelini beans
- Pepper and salt
- ½ tsp. thyme
- 1 tsp. basil
- 1 tsp. oregano
- 2 whole bay leave s
- 2 can beef broth
- 1 diced onion
- 4 diced celery stalks
- 2 diced carrots
- 1 pound ground beef
- 1 tbsp. extra-virgin olive oil

How it's made:

- Brown beef in a pan till fully heated. Pour into the base of your cooker.

- Pour in all remaining recipe components into cooker, minus pasta and beans.

- Set to heat on low 7-8 hours or set to heat on high 3-4 hours. Half an hour before you serve, stir in pasta and beans.

- With pepper and salt, season mixture to achieve desired flavor and toss out bay leaves.

Mushroom Risotto

What's in it:

- ¼ C. parmesan cheese
- 1 C. peas
- Pepper and salt
- 4 C. chicken broth
- 1 ¾ C. Arborio rice
- 1 tsp. minced garlic
- 1 diced shallot
- 8 ounces sliced portabella mushrooms
- 4 tbsp. butter

How it's made:

- Melt butter and sauté garlic, shallots, and mushrooms 5 minutes till mushrooms start to brown and liquid has mainly evaporated. Pour in rice and heat 2 minutes, stirring well to coat.
- Grease cooker and pour rice mixture into it. With pepper and salt, season to achieve desired flavor.

- Stir and set to heat on high for 1 ½ hours till rice becomes softened and all liquid becomes soaked up by rice.
- When heated, mix in parmesan cheese and peas. Enjoy!

Creamy Polenta

What's in it:

- 3 ounces shredded cheese of choice
- 1 C. half and half
- 3 C. low-sodium chicken stock
- 1 C. coarse cornmeal

How it's made:

- Mix chicken stock and cornmeal within your cooker. Set to heat on low 4 hours.
- Pour in half and half and heat on high another half and hour.
- Then stir in cheese, making sure it all melts into mixture.
- Set cooker to warm and allow the polenta sit as you make the rest of the dinner.

Spanish Rice

What's in it:

- 1 can diced tomatoes
- ½ tsp. salt
- 1 tsp. cumin
- 1 tsp chili powder
- ½ C. chopped green bell pepper
- ½ C. chopped onion
- 1 C. water
- 1 C. long grain rice

How it's made:

- Grease your cooker.
- Combine all recipe components within your cooker.
- Set to heat on low 2-3 hours till rice becomes tender and liquid is absorbed.

Beef Barley Soup

What's in it:

- Pepper and salt
- ¾ C. rinsed barley
- 15 ounces can diced tomatoes
- 1 ½ tsp. thyme
- 2 quarts beef broth
- 6 minced garlic cloves
- 3 diced celery stalks
- 1 diced onion
- 4 diced carrots
- 4 diced Yukon gold potatoes
- 2 pounds beef stew meat
- 1 ½ - 2 tbsp. olive oil

How it's made:

- Season beef with pepper and salt. Add oil to a pan and sear beef on all sides. Pour beef into a cooker.
- Add a cup of broth to skillet, heating and scraping browned bits from the pan. Pour into cooker over

beef. Then add in barley, remaining broth, tomatoes, thyme, garlic, celery, carrots, onions, and potatoes.

- Set to heat on high 4 hours. With pepper and salt, season to achieve desired flavor.
- Serve with a sprinkle of thyme and parsley.

Buffalo Chicken Pasta

What's in it:

- 16 ounces fettuccine noodles
- 1 tbsp. water
- 1 tbsp. cornstarch
- 1 tsp. salt
- 1 tsp. garlic powder
- 2 tbsp. dry ranch dressing mix
- ½ C. buffalo wing sauce
- 1 ½ C. shredded cheddar cheese
- 8 ounces cream cheese
- 24 ounces chicken broth
- 3 boneless skinless chicken breasts

How it's made:

- Pour salt, garlic powder, ranch mix, ¼ cup of buffalo wing sauce, and chicken broth into a cooker.
- Set to heat on high 4 hours or set to heat on low 8 hours.

- Take out chicken and shred with forks. Pour in remaining buffalo wing sauce, stirring to coat chicken. Set to the side.
- Mix cold water and cornstarch together, then pour into cooker. Combine everything together. Place chicken back into noodles. Heat for another hour, making sure to stir another 15 minutes.

Cheesy Garlic Parmesan Spinach Orzo

What's in it:

- ½ C. shredded parmesan cheese + more for topping
- 2/3 C. chopped spinach
- 1 C. half and half
- Pepper and salt
- 2 tsp. flour
- 2 ½ tsp. minced garlic
- 2 tbsp. olive oil
- 1 ½ C. orzo pasta

How it's made:

- Prepare orzo according to package instructions. Drain and set to the side.
- Warm up oil and sauté pepper, salt, and garlic 1 minute till fragrant.
- Mix in flour and add ¼ cup of half and half, whisking to work out lumps. Add remaining half and half. Simmer 8 minutes till sauce becomes thicker.
- Add spinach and orzo mixture to a cooker and set to heat on high 1 hour.
- Serve with sprinkle of parmesan cheese.

Chicken and Mushroom Stroganoff

What's in it:

- 1 pound egg noodles
- Parsley
- Pepper and salt
- 10.5 ounce can cream of chicken soup
- 1 package of onion soup mix
- 8 ounces softened cream cheese
- 8 ounces slice mushrooms
- 4 boneless skinless cubed chicken breasts

How it's made:

- Grease cooker and place chicken into it.
- Mix onion mix, cream of chicken soup, cream cheese, and mushrooms together. Pour over top of chicken.
- Set to heat on low 4-6 hours or set to heat on high 3-4 hours.
- Serve with pepper, salt, and topped with parsley.

Low-Carb Lasagna

What's in it:

- 8 ounces shredded mozzarella cheese
- 16 ounces low-fat cottage cheese
- 1 diced red bell pepper
- 1 diced red onion
- 16 ounces tomato-based pasta sauce
- Salt
- 2 eggs
- 1 eggplant
- 2 zucchinis

To serve:

- Parsley or basil
- Parmesan cheese

How it's made:

- Slice zucchinis and eggplant lengthwise into ¼" "noodles". Spread out onto paper towels and sprinkle with salt. Patiently allow to stand 15 minutes and then process to use paper towels to dry off.

- Grease your cooker and spread ½ of tomato sauce into the base of it in a thin layer.

- Mix eggs and cottage cheese together.

- Layer eggplant noodles, then 1/3 of cottage cheese mixture, 1/3 onions and belle peppers, 1/3 mozzarella cheese and then ½ cup of tomato sauce.

- Create second layer by adding zucchini noodles, remaining tomato sauce, peppers and onions, cottage cheese, and mozzarella cheese.

- Set to heat on high for 2-3 hours till eggplant becomes tender.

- When serving, top with a sprinkle of parmesan cheese and desired herbs.

Cilantro Lime Rice

What's in it:

- 2 tbsp. lime juice
- ½ C. chopped cilantro
- 1-2 tbsp. butter
- Pepper and salt
- 1 can black beans
- 3 C. low-sodium chicken broth
- 1 ½ C. long grained rice
- 1 tsp. cumin
- 3 minced cloves garlic
- 1-2 chopped jalapeno peppers
- ½ C. chopped red onion
- 2 tbsp. olive oil

How it's made:

- Warm up olive oil and sauté jalapenos and red onion together 3-5 minutes till tenderized. Add in cumin and garlic, sautéing 30 seconds. Then pour in rice and sauté 10 seconds.

- Add this mixture along with green chilies, chicken broth, and beans, along with remaining recipe components, into a cooker. Set to heat on high 3-4 hours.

- Season with pepper and salt when serving and a splash of lime juice.

Three Cheese Jalapeno Bacon Mac n' Cheese

What's in it:

- 1 C. shredded white cheddar
- 1 C. shredded sharp cheddar
- 1 C. shredded gouda cheese
- ¼ tsp. white pepper
- ½ tsp. onion powder
- ¼ C. + 2 tbsp. unsalted butter
- ½ C. sour cream
- 12 ounces condensed cheddar cheese soup
- 2 minced jalapeno peppers
- 6 slices bacon
- 12 ounces box rotini pasta corkscrews

How it's made:

- Prepare pasta according to package instructions, but take out about 2 minutes before totally heated. You want it to be al dente. Drain and toss with butter to prevent noodles from sticking together. Set to the side.

- Fry bacon till crispy and put on paper towels. Set to the side.
- Sauté jalapenos for 2 minutes in the bacon fat and set to the side.
- In a pan, heat ¼ C. unsalted butter, sour cream, and condensed cheddar soup till smooth, whisking to combine. Then stir in white pepper and onion powder.
- Grease your cooker. Add jalapenos and cheese sauce first, stir and then pour pasta in. Toss till evenly coated.
- Set the cooker to heat on high 1 hour.
- Chop bacon once cooker and add to mac n' cheese after an hour of heating. Heat for another 10 minutes once you have added bacon.
- Devour!

Mushroom and Wild Rice Pilaf

What's in it:

- Pepper and salt
- 2 C. reduced sodium vegetable stock
- 6 diced green onions
- 4 ounces diced mushrooms
- 1 C. wild rice
- ¼ C. unsalted butter

How it's made:

- Warm butter and toast wild rice till just browned. Pour in green onion and mushrooms and sauté 2-3 minutes.
- Pour mushroom mixture into your cooker along with vegetable stock.
- Set to heat on high 3 hours.
- With pepper and salt, season to achieve desired taste. Serve warm!

Chapter 5: Meat

Ultimate Slow Cooker Pot Roast

What's in it:

- 2 tbsp. cold water
- 2 tbsp. cornstarch
- 2 C. beef broth
- 2 minced cloves of garlic
- 2 pounds peeled/cut into chunks Yukon potatoes
- 1 pound peeled/cut into chunks carrots
- 1 tsp. thyme
- 1 tsp. pepper
- 2 tsp. salt
- 2 tbsp. olive oil
- 4-5 pound chuck roast

How it's made:

- Season roast with thyme, pepper, sand salt.
- Warm up a pan with oil and brown roast 4-5 minutes per side till browned.
- Add garlic, potatoes, and carrots to your cooker. Put chuck roast on top of veggies. Then pour in beef broth.

- Set to heat on low 8-10 hours or set to heat on high 5-6 hours.
- During the last hour of heating, combine water and cornstarch and then pour into cooker. This will help the sauce to thicken.
- To serve, cut and plate roast with veggies and top with gravy and parsley.

Brown Sugar Pineapple Ham

What's in it:

- 1 can pineapple tidbits
- ½ C. maple syrup
- 3 C. brown sugar
- 1 heated spiral bone-in ham

How it's made:

- Spread out 1 ½ cups of brown sugar into the base of your cooker. Put ham over the top of sugar and pull apart the slices a bit.
- Pour maple syrup over ham, letting it drizzle down in-between the slices.
- Pour can of pineapple tidbits into cooker, ensuring that some remain on top of ham. Sprinkle remaining brown sugar over ham.
- Set to heat on high 3 ½ - 4 hours or set to heat on low 6-7 hours.

Broccoli Beef

What's in it:

- 2 tbsp. cornstarch + 4 tbsp. cold water
- 4 C. broccoli florets
- ¼ tsp. red chili flakes
- 1 tbsp. minced garlic
- 1 tbsp. sesame oil
- 1/3 C. brown sugar
- 2/3 C. low-sodium soy sauce
- 1 C. beef broth
- 1 ½ pound flank steak (thinly sliced/chopped into 2" pieces)

How it's made:

- Grease inside of your cooker. Then add chili flakes, garlic, sesame oil, brown sugar, soy sauce, beef broth, and steak to cooker.
- Set to heat on high 2-3 hours or set to heat on low 4-5 hours.

- Before serving, open cooker. Whisk water and cornstarch together and add to cooker. Stir well. Heat another 20-25 minutes.
- To serve, microwave broccoli 3 minutes. Drain and stir into cooker. Eat!

Pot Roast Chicken

What's in it:

- 2 tsp. salt
- 2 tsp. paprika
- 1 tsp. onion powder
- ½ tsp. thyme
- 1 minced garlic cloves
- ½ tsp. pepper
- 1 whole 4-6 pound chicken with giblets removed

How it's made:

- Rinse chicken thoroughly inside and out. Dry and set to the side.
- Combine all seasonings. Rub seasoning mixture into chicken with hands, making sure to get under the skin as well.
- Place chicken into cooker. Set to heat on low 8 hours.
- Once heated, take out of cooker and eat with veggies and potatoes.
- To make gravy, utilize heating liquids. Stir cornstarch and water together and add to a pan. Mix

in some heating liquids and heat to boiling. Whisk constantly and season as needed. Serve ladled over the top of chicken and potatoes. Enjoy!

Easy BBQ Ribs

What's in it:

- 2-3 C. BBQ sauce of choice
- ½ tbsp. pepper
- 2 tbsp. brown sugar
- 2 tbsp. paprika
- 1 tbsp. salt
- 5 pounds baby back ribs

How it's made:

- Place ribs into the base of your cooker along with seasonings and BBQ sauce. Rub into meat well.
- Set to heat on low 6-8 hours. Meat should fall off bone.
- I personally like to stick my ribs into the oven when done in cooker for 5 minutes to caramelize the BBQ sauce. Devour!

Beef Tips and Gravy

What's in it:

Beef Tips:

- 4-6 minced cloves of garlic
- 1 chopped onion
- ½ tsp. pepper
- 1 tsp. salt
- 1 ½ pounds stew meat
- 1 tbsp. olive oil

Gravy:

- ¼ tsp. thyme
- ¼ tsp. oregano
- ½ tsp. paprika
- ½ tsp. parsley
- 1 ½ tsp. sugar
- 1 ½ tsp. beef bouillon
- 1 tsp. Dijon mustard
- 1 tbsp. low-sodium soy sauce

- 4 C. low-sodium beef broth
- ½ C. all-purpose flour
- 1 tbsp. butter

How it's made:

- Toss meat with ½ tsp pepper and 1 tsp. salt. Warm up oil. Working in batches, heat meat 2 minutes till seared nicely. Pour beef into your cooker.
- Mix a tbsp of butter to remaining juices in the skillet from meat. Whisk flour till dissolved. Heat to boiling and let simmer till mixture becomes thick. Pour into cooker and combine well.
- Set to heat on high 3-4 hours or set to heat on low 5-7 hours. Beef will be tenderized! Season with pepper and salt. Consume with rice, pasta, or potatoes!

Honey Pork Roast

What's in it:

- 2/3 C. grated parmesan cheese
- ¼ C. soy sauce
- 2 tbsp. olive oil
- ½ C. honey
- 2 tbsp. minced garlic
- ¾ tsp. salt
- ½ tsp. pepper
- 2 tbsp. basil
- 2 tbsp. oregano
- 3-4 pounds pork loin roast

How it's made:

- Place pork loin roast into the base of your cooker.
- Mix parmesan cheese, soy sauce, honey, garlic, pepper, salt, basil, and oregano together well. Pour mixture into cooker over meat.
- Set to heat on low 6-8 hours.

- Take out meat and shred. Pour some of the reserved heating juices from cooker into a pan. Heat to boiling and simmer till thickened.
- Pour sauce over shredded pork and enjoy!

Italian Beef Sandwiches

What's in it:

- 12 ounces sliced pepperoncini
- 2 sliced yellow onions
- 2 sliced green bell peppers
- 15 ounce jar tomato sauce
- 2 tsp. Italian seasoning
- 1 tsp. garlic powder
- 1 tsp. pepper
- 2 tsp. salt
- 4 pounds boneless beef chuck pot roast

To serve:

- 20 slices provolone cheese
- 10 crusty sandwich rolls (cut in half and toasted)

How it's made:

- Grease your cooker.
- Drain pepperoncinis, making sure to keep about 3 tbsp of liquid.

- Mix Italian seasoning, garlic powder, pepper, and salt together.
- Cut fat from roast and season all sides with about 1/3 of seasoning mixture.
- Place roast in cooker and add tomato sauce to meat. Top with pepperoncinis, onions, and bell peppers. Sprinkle with remaining seasoning mixture and top with reserved pepperoncini liquid.
- Set to heat on low 10-12 hours or set to heat on high 5-6 hours.
- Ensure oven is preheated to 250 degrees.
- Shred meat with forks. Cut rolls in half and toast in a pan. Place beef mixture with peppers and onions onto the base half of rolls. Place provolone cheese on top and other half of rolls. Pop in the oven for a few minutes to melt cheese. Devour!

BBQ Beef Brisket

What's in it:

- 18 ounces BBQ sauce of choice
- 3 tbsp. Worcestershire sauce
- 1 ½ tsp. liquid smoke
- 1 C. water
- ½ tsp. cumin
- 1 tsp. garlic powder
- 1 tsp. onion powder
- 2 tsp. salt
- 2 tsp. pepper
- 1 tbsp. paprika
- 1 tbsp. thyme
- 2-3 pounds beef brisket

How it's made:

- Mix cumin, garlic powder, onion powder, pepper, salt, paprika, and thyme together. Rub this mixture over brisket.
- Pour 1 cup water within base of your cooker. Then carefully place brisket into water. Pour

Worcestershire sauce and liquid smoke into water around meat. Set to heat on low 12 hours.

- When done, trim fat from brisket and shred meat. Place shredded meat back into cooker and add BBQ sauce on top. Stir and heat another half an hour till sauce is warmed through.

Mongolian Chicken

What's in it:

- ½ tsp. garlic powder
- ½ tsp. ground ginger
- ½ C. dark brown sugar
- ¼ C. soy sauce
- 5 bone-in, skin on chicken thighs

How it's made:

- Combine all recipe components together minus chicken. Set chicken into the base of cooker, skin side up. Add mixture over chicken.
- Set to heat on high 4 hours or set to heat on low 8 hours.
- Garnish with green onions and sesame seeds.

Chicken Cordon Bleu Casserole

What's in it:

- 1/3 C. melted butter
- 1 package cornbread
- 1 package sliced Swiss cheese
- ½ pound ham slices
- 2 pounds boneless skinless chicken breasts
- ¼ tsp. garlic powder
- ¼ tsp. pepper
- ½ tsp. oregano
- ¼ C. milk
- 1 can cream of chicken soup

How it's made:

- Whisk garlic powder, pepper, oregano, milk, and chicken soup together. Set to the side.
- Place chicken breasts into the base of your cooker. Place ham in an even layer over the top. Then place Swiss cheese in an even layer over ham. Top with soup mixture. Spread out to coat. Sprinkle cornbread mix over everything, along with melted butter.
- Set to heat on low 5 hours.

Cubed Steak with Gravy

What's in it:

- 3 tbsp. cold water
- 3 tbsp. cornstarch
- 1 ½ - 2 pounds cube steak
- ½ C. water
- 1 can French onion soup
- 1 can cream of chicken soup
- 1 packet au just gravy mix

How it's made:

- Pour water, packet of au jus, French onion soup, and cream of chicken soup into the base of your cooker. Combine well.
- Place cubed steak into gravy mixture.
- Set to heat on low 6-8 hours.
- Once heated, to make gravy, whisk cold water and cornstarch together and add to cooker. Set cooker on high for half an hour till gravy becomes thick.

Slow Cooker Taco Meat

What's in it:

- ½ tsp. pepper
- 1 tsp. smoked paprika
- 1 ½ tsp. garlic powder
- 1 ½ tsp. salt
- 1 tsp. cumin
- 1 diced onion
- 1 C. green chilies
- 1 ½ C. diced tomatoes with juice
- 2 pounds ground beef

How it's made:

- Pour all recipe components into your cooker.
- Set to heat on high 2-4 hours till meat is thoroughly heated. If you plan to wait to devour, turn cooker to the 'warm' setting to keep toasty.
- Serve with tortillas and favorite taco toppings.

Cajun Chicken and Rice

What's in it:

- 2 C. chicken broth
- 1 chopped bell pepper
- 1 ½ C. rinsed rice
- 1 tbsp. tomato paste
- 3 minced cloves garlic
- 1 diced onion
- 1 tbsp. olive oil
- 1 tbsp. Cajun seasoning
- 1 pound chicken breast

How it's made:

- Slice chicken breast in lengthwise in half. Season on both sides with Cajun seasoning.
- Warm oil and sauté onion and garlic together till just browned. Stir in tomato paste.
- Place chicken into cooker along with tomato mixture and remaining recipe components. Set to heat on high 3-4 hours.

- Take out chicken and shred meat using forks. Then add chicken back into pot to combine with other ingredients. Adjust seasonings to achieve desired flavor.

- Serve topped with a sprinkle of cilantro.

Lentil Sloppy Joes

What's in it:

- 3-4 C. vegetable broth
- Pinch of pepper and salt
- 1 tsp. paprika
- 1 tbsp. chili powder
- 2 tbsp. mustard
- 2 tbsp. hot sauce
- 2 tbsp. maple syrup
- ½ C. ketchup
- 1 can tomato sauce
- ½ C. quinoa
- 1 ½ C. brown lentils
- 2 minced garlic cloves
- 1 C. chopped onions
- 1 C. chopped mushrooms
- 1 C. chopped carrots

How it's made:

- Pour all recipe components into your cooker. Combine well to incorporate.

- Set to heat on high 2-3 hours or set to heat on low 4-6 hours.

- Serve warm on a biscuit or bun or paired with spaghetti squash. Enjoy!

Chapter 6: Seafood

Clam Chowder

What's in it:

- 2 slices chopped bacon
- 1 C. whole milk
- 1 C. half and half
- 3 tbsp. all-purpose flour
- 2 tbsp. butter
- ¼ tsp. pepper
- ¼ tsp. salt
- ½ tsp. thyme
- 8 ounces clam juice
- 3 cans chopped clams
- 3 peeled/diced russet potatoes
- 1 diced onion

How it's made:

- Add potatoes and onions to your cooker. Add 2 cans of clams with the juice and 1 can without the juice. Throw away any remaining juice. Add pepper, salt, thyme, and clam juice to cooker. Combine well.
- Set to heat on high for 4 hours.

- Melt butter and add flour, stirring well till thickened. Gradually add in half and half and milk, continually stirring till nice and thick.
- Pour milk mixture into slow heat and heat on low for half an hour.
- Spoon into serving bowls, top with bacon and serve with saltine or oyster crackers.

BBQ Shrimp

What's in it:

- Pepper and salt
- 1 C. BBQ sauce of choice
- 2 tsp. minced garlic
- 2 tbsp. Worcestershire sauce
- 3 tbsp. butter
- 2 pounds peeled/deveined shrimp

How it's made:

- Toss shrimp into the base of your cooker. Add BBQ sauce, garlic, Worcestershire sauce, and butter and gently toss.
- Set to heat on low for 1 hour.
- Serve BBQ shrimp with toasted French bread, veggies, and lemon wedges.

Indian Fish Curry

What's in it:

- 3 tbsp. chopped cilantro
- 2 pounds white fish fillets of choice (halibut, cod, or tilapia)
- Salt
- 1 tbsp. sugar
- 2 chopped tomatoes
- 2 tsp. turmeric
- 2 tsp. brown mustard seeds
- 2 tsp. coriander
- 1 tbsp. cumin
- 1" peeled/grated ginger
- 2 hot green chilies
- 2 minced garlic cloves
- 1 chopped yellow onion
- 1/3 C. olive oil

How it's made:

- Put the flameproof insert into your cooker upon the stove. Warm up oil till hot and sauté onion till golden. Then mix in turmeric, mustard, coriander, cumin, ginger, chilies, and garlic, stirring and heating 1 minute till fragrant. Add salt, sugar, and tomatoes. Heat till tomatoes start to release juices. Pour in 1 ½ cups water to deglaze, scraping browned bits. Heat to boiling point.

- Place insert back into cooker. Set to heat on low 2 hours. Set a timer to check sauce halfway through. If it seems too thick, stir in ½ cup more water.

- Add fish to cooker and coat with sauce. Heat another half an hour.

- Serve topped with cilantro. Enjoy!

Slow Cooker Salmon

What's in it:

- 1 – 1 ½ C. liquid of choice (Cider, beer, wine, broth water, or a mix)
- Slice veggies with aromatics (celery, onions, fennel, etc.)
- Sliced lemon
- Spices of choice
- Pepper and salt
- 1 – 2 pounds salmon fillets with skin still intact

How it's made:

- Cut up salmon fillets into pieces that are about the same size as your cooker. Season with pepper and salt, along with other seasonings you choose.
- With foil, line your cooker. Place veggies of choice into the base of cooker first. Then place salmon over top with the skin side down.
- Pour choice of heating liquid over top of salmon and veggies. Set cooker to heat on low 1-2 hours. Check fish every 20 minutes or so till its done heating.
- Lift salmon by edges of foil from cooker. Serve!

Shrimp Scampi

What's in it:

- 1 pound peeled/deveined raw shrimp
- Pepper and salt
- ½ freshly squeezed lemon
- 2 tbsp. parsley
- 1 tbsp. minced garlic
- 2 tbsp. butter
- 2 tbsp. olive oil
- ¼ C. chicken broth

How it's made:

- Add pepper, salt, lemon juice, parsley, garlic, butter, olive oil, and broth to cooker. Place shrimp into cooker and stir well to incorporate.
- Set to heat on high 1 ½ hours or set to heat on low 2 ½ hours.
- Serve with your favorite noodles or devour as is!

New Orleans Spicy BBQ Shrimp

What's in it:

- 1 chopped green onion
- 1 ½ pounds unpeeled large shrimp
- Pepper and salt
- Juice of 1 lemon
- 1 tbsp. hot pepper sauce
- ¼ C. Worcestershire sauce
- ½ C. unsalted butter
- 1 tsp. Cajun seasoning
- 2 minced cloves garlic

How it's made:

- Pour lemon juice, hot pepper sauce, Worcestershire sauce, butter, Cajun seasoning, and garlic into the base of your cooker and stir well. Set to heat on high for half an hour.
- Rinse and drain shrimp.
- Spoon out about ½ of the sauce within your cooker and set to the side.

- Put shrimp in cooker and drizzle reserved sauce over it. Stir to evenly coat.
- Set to heat on high for 30 minutes till shrimp are opaque in color.
- Sprinkle green onions when serving.

Maple Salmon

What's in it:

- 1 tsp. minced ginger root
- 2 tsp. crushed garlic
- ¼ C. soy sauce
- 1/8 C. lime juice
- ½ C. maple syrup
- 6 salmon fillets

How it's made:

- Place salmon into the base of your cooker.
- Combine all of remaining recipe components till incorporated and pour over salmon fillets.
- Set to heat for 1 hour on high.
- Can be served warm or cold with pasta, rice, or salad!

Salmon Curry

What's in it:

- ¼ tsp. salt
- ½ tsp. pepper
- 1 tsp. turmeric
- 2 tsp. smoke paprika
- 1 tsp. chili powder
- 1 ½ tsp. cumin
- 1 ½ tsp. coriander
- 12 ounce can tomato paste
- ½ C. vegetable stock
- 2 cans coconut milk
- 2 chopped carrots
- 3 chopped celery stalks
- 2 tbsp. grated ginger
- 6 chopped garlic cloves
- 1 chopped onion
- 6 pieces salmon, skin removed

How it's made:

- Pour coconut milk into cooker, then tomato paste, vegetable stock, paprika, turmeric, chili, cumin, and coriander. Then pepper and salt. Combine all ingredients together to incorporate.
- Place salmon into mixture in cooker. Then pour carrots, celery, ginger, garlic, and onions over top.
- Set to heat on high 2 ½ - 3 hours.
- Serve with rice!

Lemon Dill Halibut

What's in it:

- 1 ½ tsp. dill
- 1 tbsp. olive oil
- 1 tbsp. lemon juice
- Pepper and salt
- 12 ounces wild halibut

How it's made:

- Tear off a piece of foil and place halibut in the middle of it. Season with pepper and salt.
- Whisk dill, olive oil, and lemon juice together and drizzle over halibut.
- Crimp edges of foil together to create a foil packet. Stick packet into the base of your cooker and set to heat on high for 1 ½ - 2 hours.
- To serve, take packet out of cooker and top halibut with lemon juice. Enjoy!

Red Curry with Cod

What's in it:

- Pepper and salt
- 1 pound cod fish fillet
- 12 ounces julienne carrots
- 1 sliced red bell pepper
- 1 tsp. garlic powder
- 1 tsp. ginger
- 1 tbsp. curry powder
- 3 tbsp. red curry pasta
- 2 15 ounce cans coconut milk

How it's made:

- Pour in coconut milk, garlic powder, ginger, curry powder, and curry paste into the base of your cooker. Mix well to combine.
- Add in carrots and bell pepper slices and then place cod into the sauce over veggies.
- Set to heat on low 2 hours.

- Once heated, break cod into bite sized pieces. Season with pepper and salt if needed. Eat with rice and top with green onion and/or cilantro.

Coconut Cilantro Curry Shrimp

What's in it:

- ¼ C. cilantro
- 2 ½ tsp. lemon garlic seasoning
- 1-2 tbsp. red curry paste
- 15 ounces water
- 30 ounces light coconut milk
- 1 pound shrimp, shells intact

Lemon Garlic Seasoning:

- 1 tsp. pepper
- 1 ½ tsp. onion powder
- 2 tsp. salt
- 1 tbsp. garlic powder
- Zest of 5 lemons

How it's made:

- Mix cilantro, lemon garlic seasoning, red curry sauce, water, and coconut milk within the base of your cooker.
- Set to heat on high 2 hours.

- Place shrimp into cooker and heat 15-30 more minutes till shrimp is completely heated.
- Serve topped with cilantro.

Cilantro Lime Fish Tacos

What's in it:

- Salt
- 2 tbsp. lime juice
- 1 ½ tbsp. cilantro
- ½ tsp. minced garlic
- 1 can Rotel
- 6 fish fillets of choice (tilapia, salmon, cod, etc.)

How it's made:

- Place fish fillets into the base of your cooker. Cover with salt, lime juice, cilantro, garlic, and Rotel.
- Set to heat on high 4 hours.
- Flake fish with a folk and combine thoroughly with other heated components.
- Spoon onto soft taco shells and enjoy!

Shrimp and Cheese Grits

What's in it:

- 1 tbsp. chopped chives
- 1 pound heated/peeled/deveined shrimp
- 2 tsp. hot sauce
- 2 tbsp. unsalted butter
- 1 C. shredded cheese of choice
- ¼ C. heavy cream
- Pepper and salt
- 2 C. grits

How it's made:

- Within your cooker, mix 1 ½ tsp. salt, 8 cups of water and grits together. Set to heat on low 6 hours till liquid becomes absorbed.
- Add in hot sauce, butter, cheese, and cream. Stir till cheese melts. Season with pepper and salt to achieve desired flavor.
- Put shrimp on top of mixture and heat 5-10 minutes to warm shrimp thoroughly.
- Serve topped with chives.

Fire Roasted Shrimp Tacos

What's in it:

- 1-2 tbsp. olive oil
- 3-4 tbsp. chopped cilantro
- ½ tsp. minced garlic
- ¼ - ½ tsp. cayenne pepper
- ½ tsp. cumin
- Dash of pepper and salt
- ½ C. chopped bell pepper
- 2 tbsp. spicy salsa
- 14.5 ounce can fire-roasted stewed tomatoes
- 11 ounces peeled/frozen raw shrimp

How it's made:

- Lay out frozen shrimp in a single layer within the base of your cooker. Drizzle with olive oil.
- Sprinkle pepper and salt around shrimp. Drain tomato juice from tomatoes and add on top of shrimp.
- Mix well and set to heat on high 2 hours or set to heat on low 3-4 hours.
- Serve with avocado, rice, and tortillas.

Low Country Boil

What's in it:

- 2 pounds unheated shrimp in shells
- 4 fresh corn cobs
- 1 pound heated kielbasa sausage
- 2 lemons
- 3-4 minced cloves of garlic
- 1 onion
- 2 celery stalks
- ¼ C. Old Bay seasoning
- 1 bottle beer of choice
- 5 C. water
- 1 ½ pounds small red potatoes

How it's made:

- Grease your cooker. Then pour in garlic, Old Bay seasoning, water, and beer into cooker. Combine well.
- Cut lemons in half and squeeze juice into cooker and then put lemon into liquid. Cut potatoes in half, quarter your onion, cut celery into 1" pieces and cut

corn cobs into 3" chunks. Place celery, onion, and potatoes into cooker.

- Set to heat on low 4-5 hours. Then add corn and sausage to cooker and heat another 2 hours.
- Increase heat to high and add shrimp to cooker. Heat 30-40 minutes till shrimp are completely heated.

Chapter 7: Vegetables

Cheddar Corn

What's in it:

- ¼ tsp. pepper
- ½ tsp. salt
- ¼ C. heavy cream
- ¼ C. butter
- 1 C. shredded cheddar cheese
- 8 ounces cream cheese
- 12 ounces frozen corn
- 16 ounces frozen corn

How it's made:

- Pour all recipe components into cooker.
- Set to heat on low for 3 ½ - 4 hours. Stir well before devouring!

Slow Cooker Mashed Potatoes

What's in it:

- ½ C. unsalted butter
- 3 – 3 ½ C. milk
- Pepper
- 1 tsp. salt
- 3-4 cloves garlic
- 5 pounds russet potatoes

How it's made:

- Peel and cut up potatoes. Grease your cooker and add in potatoes. Sprinkle seasonings over potatoes. Season liberally with pepper and salt. Pour in milk and stir well.
- Set to heat on high 4-5 hours till potatoes become soft and tender. Then turn cooker to warm.
- Melt butter in a pan and stir in to cups milk.
- Discard garlic cloves and mash potato mixture. Once smooth, stir in warmed butter mixture. Allow time for potatoes to soak up liquid. Season with pepper and salt to achieve desired flavor.

Garlic Parmesan Spaghetti Squash

What's in it:

- Pepper and salt
- ½ C. grated parmesan cheese
- ¼ C. heavy cream
- 3 minced cloves garlic
- 6 tbsp. unsalted butter
- 1 spaghetti squash

How it's made:

- With a knife, pierce spaghetti squash. Place in cooker and set to heat on high 3-4 hours or on low 6-8 hours.
- When squash becomes tender, take out of cooker and let heat a bit. Slice lengthwise and take out seeds. Scrape flesh to create long strands.
- Place flesh of squash back into your cooker and set it to low. Ad butter, garlic, and cream. Combine well. Heat on low till creamy and thickened.
- Add parmesan cheese and season with pepper and salt.
- When serving, top with parsley and a sprinkle or two of parmesan cheese.

Butternut Squash and Apples

What's in it:

- 1 ½ tsp. nutmeg
- 1 tbsp. cinnamon
- 1 C. dried cranberries
- 4 cored/sliced apples of choice
- 1 package diced butternut squash

How it's made:

- Pour all recipe components into the base of your cooker.
- Set to heat on high 2-3 hours, stirring on occasion till squash is tender.
- Once softened, switch cooker to warm till ready to serve.

Corn and Potato Chowder

What's in it:

- Pepper and salt
- 2 C. half and half
- 4 C. chicken stock
- ½ tsp. seasoned salt
- 6-8 crushed cloves of garlic
- 1 C. chopped celery
- 1 chopped yellow onion
- 8 C. kernel corn
- 2 ½ pounds russet potatoes
- 8 ounces heated/crumbled bacon

How it's made:

- Dump all recipe components minus half and half into your cooker.
- Set to heat on low 10 hours or set to heat on high 6 hours.
- With an immersion blender, pour in half and half into mixture and blender till creamy.

- Heat another 15 minutes till everything is heated through. Season with pepper and salt.

Balsamic Brussels Sprouts

What's in it:

- ¼ C. grated parmesan cheese
- ½ C. chopped pecans
- ¼ tsp. pepper
- ½ tsp. salt
- 2 tbsp. olive oil
- 3 tbsp. pure maple syrup
- ¼ C. balsamic vinegar
- 3 pounds trimmed/halved Brussels sprouts

How it's made:

- Place Brussels sprouts into the base of your cooker. Then mix in pepper, salt, olive oil, maple syrup, and vinegar.
- Set to heat on high for 1 – 1 ½ hours or set to heat on low for 2 – 2 ½ hours till the sprouts become tenderized and have a bit of a crunch.
- Mix in parmesan cheese and pecans and pour entire mixture into a serving platter.

- Serve warm with a drizzle of balsamic glaze from base of cooker.

Onion Potatoes

What's in it:

- 1/3 C. olive oil
- 1 packet onion soup mix
- ¼ tsp. pepper
- ¼ tsp. garlic powder
- 2 pounds sliced russet potatoes

How it's made:

- Place potatoes into the base of cooker. Mix onion soup mix, pepper, and garlic powder together and sprinkle over potatoes. Drizzle with olive oil.
- Set to heat on high for 4 hours.

Honey Cinnamon Carrots

What's in it:

- 1 tsp. cinnamon
- ½ tsp. vanilla extract
- ¼ C. honey
- 1 tbsp. bourbon whiskey
- ¾ tsp. salt
- ¼ C. melted butter
- 2 pounds baby carrots

How it's made:

- Pour carrots into the base of your cooker.
- Melt butter and mix in bourbon and salt. Pour bourbon mixture over carrots and toss to evenly coat.
- Set to heat on low for 6-8 hours or set to heat on high for 3-4 hours till carrots become tender.
- Mix vanilla extract and honey together and drizzle over carrots. Sprinkle with cinnamon.

    Set cooker to warm to keep carrots toasty till ready to eat. Enjoy!

Cabbage Roll Casserole

What's in it:

- 1 C. unheated white rice
- ½ tsp. pepper
- ½ tsp. salt
- 1 tbsp. beef bouillon
- 1 tbsp. Worcestershire sauce
- 1 tsp. minced garlic
- 2 cans tomato sauce
- 1 can diced tomatoes
- 1 chopped onion
- 1 chopped green pepper
- 1 chopped head of cabbage
- 1 pound ground beef

How it's made:

- Place all recipe components into your cooker, minus the rice. Combine well to incorporate.
- Set to heat on high for 1 hour. Then add rice, stir and heat another 2 hours.

Easy Slow Cooker Veggies

What's in it:

- Seasonings of choice (I love Cajun!)
- Pepper and salt
- 3 tbsp. butter
- 8 C. frozen or fresh veggies of choice (cauliflower, green beans, broccoli, etc.)

How it's made:

- Toss all veggies, pepper, and salt within the base of your cooker.
- Top with slices of butter.
- Set to heat on high 2 hours.

Beef Vegetable Stew

What's in it:

- 2 C. peas
- ¾ C. cold water
- ¼ C. cornstarch
- ¼ tsp. pepper
- ¾ tsp. salt
- 1 tsp. sugar
- 1 minced garlic clove
- 2 tsp. beef bouillon granules
- 1 tbsp. browning sauce
- 2 tbsp. Worcestershire sauce
- 1 chopped celery rib
- 1 chopped onion
- 1 can condensed soup
- 1 - ½ C. baby carrots
- 3 C. water
- 3 peeled/cubed potatoes
- 1 ½ pounds boneless beef chuck roast (cut into 1" cubes)

How it's made:

- Pour pepper, salt, sugar, garlic, bouillon granules, browning sauce, Worcestershire sauce , celery, onion, soup, carrots, water, potatoes, and beef into cooker.
- Set to heat on low 6-8 hours till meat becomes tender.
- Mix cold water and cornstarch together and then mix into stew.
- Heat another 30 minutes.

Lentil and Vegetable Soup

What's in it:

- 6 ½ C. vegetable stock
- ¼ tsp. cayenne pepper
- ½ tsp. garlic salt
- ½ tsp. paprika
- 1 tsp. salt
- 1 tsp. parsley
- ½ chopped onion
- 2 pressed garlic cloves
- 1 chopped jalapeno
- 2 peeled/chopped russet potatoes
- ½ chopped bunch of kale
- 2 chopped celery stalks
- 1 chopped red bell pepper
- 4 peeled/chopped carrots
- 1 ½ C. red lentils

How it's made:

- Pour all recipe components into your cooker.

- Set to heat on high 5 hours or set to heat on low 8 hours.
- Serve with a nice dollop of sour cream and crusty bread.

Pumpkin Applesauce

What's in it:

- Brown sugar
- ½ C. apple juice
- 1 tsp. vanilla extract
- ½ tsp. ground cloves
- ½ tsp. nutmeg
- 2 tsp. cinnamon
- 1 can pumpkin puree
- 8 gala apples

How it's made:

- Peel, core and slice gala apples. Place into cooker. Then pour in apple juice, vanilla, cloves, nutmeg, cinnamon, and pumpkin puree. Combine well.
- Set to heat on high 5 hours or set to heat on low 8 hours.
- When done heating, whisk till you reach desired smoothness. Add brown sugar to achieve desired flavor.

Sweet Potato Casserole

What's in it:

Sweet Potato Puree:

- 1 beaten egg
- 1 tsp. vanilla extract
- 1/3 C. pure maple syrup
- 3 tbsp. coconut oil
- ¼ C. milk
- 3 ½ pounds sweet potatoes

Pecan Topping:

- 1/8 tsp. salt
- 1/8 tsp. nutmeg
- ½ tsp. cinnamon
- 2 tbsp. almond flour
- 2-3 tbsp. pure maple syrup
- 2 tbsp. melted coconut oil
- 1 1/3 C. chopped toasted pecans

How it's made:

- Grease inside of cooker. Pour sweet potatoes into cooker and set to heat on high 2-3 hours till potatoes become softened.

- With an immersion blender, mash sweet potatoes directly in cooker. Mix in egg, vanilla, maple syrup, coconut oil, and milk.

- Mix salt, nutmeg, cinnamon, flour, maple syrup, oil, and pecans together in a bowl. Sprinkle pecan mixture over sweet potato mixture.

- Set to heat on high another 45 minutes to 1 ½ hours.

Ratatouille Pasta

What's in it:

- 2 C. vegetable broth
- 46 ounces Ragu roasted garlic sauce
- 10 ounces dried pasta
- 2 tbsp. chopped basil
- 1 C. chopped onion
- 1 minced garlic clove
- 2 chopped bell peppers
- 2 ½ C. sliced zucchini
- 2 ½ C. cubed eggplant

How it's made:

- Prep veggies and place in cooker. Add pasta over veggies. Sprinkle with basil and pour sauces over everything along with broth.
- Set to heat on low 2 hours. Mix well. Then heat another 2 hours till pasta is thoroughly heated.
- Sprinkle with parsley and parmesan cheese.

Chapter 8: Sauces

Homemade Slow Cooker Tomato Sauce (Made with FRESH Tomatoes!)

What's in it:

- Pepper and salt
- ½ tsp. chopped rosemary
- 1 tsp. chopped thyme
- 1 tsp. chopped oregano
- 1 tbsp. chopped basil
- 2 tbsp. chopped parsley
- 1 bay leaf
- 2 tbsp. extra virgin olive oil
- 1 chopped carrot
- 1 chopped onion
- 3 crushed cloves garlic
- ¼ C. red wine
- 5-6 pounds paste tomatoes

How it's made:

- Wash tomatoes under water. Slice them in quarters or halves and place into your cooker. Then add olive oil, wine, herbs, carrots, onion, and garlic.

- Set to heat on low 2-4 hours. Once simmering, turn off cooker. Allow to cool.

- Run cooled sauce through a strainer. Pour back into cooker and heat longer to thicken. Set cooker to low and heat 4-6 hours.

- Once thick, taste and season as desired. If you choose to add additional ingredients, do so now. Heat for 1-2 more hours if adding more desired components.

Meat Lover's Spaghetti Sauce

What's in it:

- 1 tbsp. sugar
- 1 tsp. garlic powder
- ½ tsp. oregano
- ¼ tsp. basil
- ¼ tsp. thyme leaves
- 1 can Italian-style stewed tomatoes
- 1 can Italian-style diced tomatoes
- 1 can tomato paste
- 1 can tomato sauce
- ½ tsp. marjoram
- 1 tsp. garlic powder
- 1 tsp. Italian herb seasoning
- 1 pound ground beef
- ¼ pound Italian sausage
- 2 chopped onions

How it's made:

- Warm up olive oil and sauté Italian sausage and onions together for 10 minutes till browned. Pour into cooker.

- Heat marjoram, garlic powder, Italian seasoning, and ground beef together 10 minutes till browned. Pour ground beef mixture into cooker.

- Stir in garlic powder, oregano, basil, thyme, stewed and diced tomatoes, tomato paste and sauce.

- Set to heat on low 8 hours.

- About 15 minutes before cooking is complete, mix in sugar.

Slow Cooker Marinara

What's in it:

- Pepper and salt
- 1 tbsp. balsamic vinegar
- 1 tbsp. brown sugar
- ½ tbsp. oregano
- 1 tbsp. basil
- 2 bay leaves
- ½ tbsp. minced garlic
- 1 yellow onion
- 6 ounces tomato paste
- 2 cans crushed tomatoes

How it's made:

- Cut up onion and mince garlic and put into cooker. Add pepper, oregano, basil, bay leaves, balsamic vinegar, brown sugar, tomato paste and crushed tomatoes into cooker.
- Set to heat on low 8 hours.
- Stir sauce and discard bay leaves. Season with salt.

Bolognese Sauce

What's in it:

- 1 bay leaf
- 2 cans whole peeled tomatoes
- 1 C. white wine
- 2 tsp. salt
- 1/8 tsp. nutmeg
- ½ tsp. pepper
- ½ tsp. oregano
- ½ tsp. thyme
- 2 tbsp. salt
- 1 ½ - 2 pounds ground beef
- 2-3 minced cloves garlic
- 1 chopped carrot
- 2 chopped celery stalks
- 1 chopped yellow onion
- 1 tbsp. olive oil

How it's made:

- Sauté onion, carrot, and celery till onion becomes translucent in color. Add garlic and tomato paste and heat 30 seconds. Then pour in beef, nutmeg, pepper, oregano, and thyme into cooker. Then stir in milk and bring to simmer. Pour mixture into cooker.

- Strain tomatoes but reserve juices. Pour tomatoes into cooker along with bay leaf. Set to heat on low 6-8 hours.

- During the last 30 minutes of heating, check sauce. Remove some liquid so that it turns creamy and thick.

- Serve over favorite pasta!

Short Rib Sauce

What's in it:

- 1 parmesan cheese rinds
- 1 bay leaf
- ¼ tsp. red pepper flakes
- ½ tsp. pepper
- ½ tsp. salt
- 2 tsp. Italian seasoning
- 3 sun-dried tomatoes
- 1 can peeled plum tomatoes
- 1 chopped celery stalk
- 1 chopped carrot
- 1 chopped onion
- Pepper and salt
- 3-4 pounds beef short ribs
- 2 tbsp. olive oil

How it's made:

- Warm up oil and season ribs with pepper and salt. Sear both sides.
- Grease a cooker and add garlic, celery, carrot, and onion. Lay ribs over top.
- Chop tomatoes and pour in with short ribs. Pour in all remaining recipe components.
- Set to heat on low 8 hours.

Chapter 9: Desserts and Sweets

Caramel Apple Crumble

What's in it:

Apples:

- 1 tsp. cinnamon
- ¼ tsp. salt
- 5 apples (peeled/sliced into chunks)
- ½ C. sugar
- 1 C. brown sugar

Topping:

- 1 tsp. vanilla extract
- 3-4 tbsp. softened butter
- ½ tsp. cinnamon
- ¼ C. flour
- 2/3 C. brown sugar
- 2/3 C. oats

How it's made:

- Combine cinnamon, salt, apples, sugar and brown sugar. Spread mixture into the base of cooker.

- Then mix topping components till combined. Sprinkle over apples.

- Set to heat on low 4 hours or set to heat on high 2 hours.

- Turn off cooker and let sit 1 hour for caramel to thicken.

Caramel Peanut Butter Hot Fudge

What's in it:

- 1 C. boiling water
- 3 tbsp. unsweetened cocoa powder
- 15-20 Rolos
- ¾ C. peanut butter
- ½ tsp. vanilla extract
- 1/3 C. vegetable oil
- 1 C. milk
- 1 tsp. baking powder
- 1 C. sugar
- 1 C. all-purpose flour

How it's made:

- Stir baking powder, ½ cup sugar, and flour together. Then stir in vanilla extract, oil, and milk till smooth. Then mix in peanut butter till incorporated.
- Grease your cooker and pour batter into the cooker. Press Rolo candies into batter.

- Whisk cocoa powder and ½ cup of remaining sugar. Gradually whisk in boiling water. Then pour water mixture over top of cake.

- Set to heat on high for 2 hours. Allow to cool for a few minutes before serving with whipped or ice cream.

Brownie Pudding

What's in it:

- 2 C. milk
- 1 package instant chocolate fudge pudding mix
- 1 box brownie mix
- Oil, water, eggs that brownie mix calls for

How it's made:

- Grease a cooker.
- Prepare brownie mix according to box instructions. Pour into cooker.
- Whisk milk and pudding mix together till smooth. Pour over brownie mix.
- Cover cooker with paper towels. Set to heat on high 2-3 hours.
- Serve with ice cream or whipped cream. Devour!

Caramel Cake

What's in it:

- 2 tbsp. butter
- ¾ C. brown sugar
- 1 ½ C. boiling water
- 3 eggs
- ½ C. vegetable oil
- 1 C. creamer, flavor of choice
- 1 yellow cake mix

How it's made:

- Grease your cooker.
- Mix eggs, oil, creamer, and cake mix together till smooth. Pour into cooker.
- Warm up water till it reaches boiling point and whisk in butter and brown sugar. Drizzle over cake batter.
- Cover cooker with paper towels and set to heat on high 1 ½ - 2 ½ hours. Begin checking on cake at 1 ½ hours. Once it starts to look like baked batter, it's close to done.
- Serve with ice cream and caramel sauce.

Cinnamon Roll Monkey Bread

What's in it:

- ½ C. melted unsalted butter
- ½ C. brown sugar
- 1 tsp. cinnamon
- ¼ C. sugar
- 2 cans cinnamon rolls

How it's made:

- Open cinnamon rolls and reserve icing packets. Cut each of the rolls into 6 pieces.
- In a Ziploc bag, pour in sugar and cinnamon. Place cut up pieces of rolls and shake till all bread is coated.
- Stir melted butter and brown sugar together.
- Grease a cooker. Place half of the dough into the base of your cooker. Then drizzle with half of melted butter mixture and then layer remaining pieces of roll and top with remaining butter mixture.
- Set to heat on high 2 hours. Edges will begin to turn brown. Shut off cooker and let sit 5 minutes. Drizzle reserved icing packets over rolls. Enjoy!

Apple Dump Cake

What's in it:

- ½ C. sliced butter
- ½ C. oats
- 1 box yellow cake mix
- 1 ½ tsp. cinnamon
- ¼ C. sugar
- 5-7 granny smith apples

How it's made:

- Peel, core, and slice apples. You want them to be both bite sized and thin.
- Grease cooker and place apples into the base of cooker. Sprinkle with sugar and ½ tsp cinnamon.
- Mix 1 tsp cinnamon, oats, and cake mix together. Sprinkle over top of apples.
- Place slices of butter on top of cake mix.
- Set to heat on high 4 hours. When butter is completely melted and the top turns golden, cake is done!

Dulce De Leche

What's in it:

- Water
- 2 can sweetened condensed milk
- 3-8 ounce jars with lids and rings

How it's made:

- Divide condensed milk among your jars. Seal with rings and put into cooker.
- Fill your cooker with water to cover about 1-2" above the tops of jars.
- Set to heat on low 10 hours.
- Remove the jars carefully with tongs and let them sit to cool to room temp.
- Chill in the fridge till you plan to use.

Caramel Blondies

What's in it:

- 1 C. boiling water
- 12 squares of caramel
- ½ C. milk
- 1 tsp. vanilla extract
- ¼ C. softened butter
- 1 C. brown sugar
- ½ tsp. salt
- 1 tsp. baking powder
- 1 C. all-purpose flour

How it's made:

- Mix salt, baking powder, and flour together.
- Cream ½ cup of brown sugar and butter till creamy. Then mix in vanilla. Add 1/3 of flour mixture and 1/3 of milk. Continue to add milk and flour till all is incorporated.
- Mix in caramels. Spread batter into the base of a cooker.

- Combine ½ cup of brown sugar with boiling water, mixing till sugar is dissolved. Pour over batter in cooker.
- Set to heat on high 2 ½ - 3 hours.
- Serve with ice cream. Indulge!

Slow Cooker Candy

What's in it:

- 1 bag caramels
- 16 ounces white almond bark + more for drizzling
- 4 C. chocolate chips
- 3 C. peanuts or other nuts of choice

How it's made:

- Chop bark into chocolate chip sized pieces.
- Pour nuts into cooker so that they cover entire base.
- Pour chocolate over nuts and layer white bark over chocolate chips.
- Set to heat on low 1-2 hours. Turn cooker off.
- Mix chocolate mixture till smooth. Then fold in caramels.
- Spoon candy mixture into mini paper liners or onto wax paper.
- Drizzle extra white bark over candies and allow candies to totally cool. Enjoy!

S'mores Brownies

What's in it:

Crust:

- ½ C. sugar
- ¾ C. melted butter
- 3 C. graham cracker crumbs

Brownies:

- 1 C. semisweet chocolate chips
- ½ tsp. salt
- ¾ tsp. baking powder
- ¼ C. unsweetened cocoa powder
- 1 ¼ C. all-purpose flour
- 3 eggs
- 1 C. sugar
- 8 ounces chopped bittersweet chocolate
- ½ C. butter

Topping:

- 10 ounces mini marshmallows
- 4 Hershey milk chocolate bars

How it's made:

- With parchment paper, line your cooker.
- Mix sugar, melted butter, and graham cracker crumbs together. Press this mixture into the base of cooker.
- Heat butter in a pan and melt bittersweet chocolate. Mix in sugar, then 1 egg at a time. Then mix in salt, baking powder, cocoa powder, and flour. Fold in chocolate chips. Spread chocolate mixture over graham cracker crust.
- Break Hershey bars apart and sprinkle over batter in cooker.
- Set to heat on low 2 – 2 ½ hours.
- Pour marshmallows on top of dessert and heat 5-10 more minutes.

Slow Cooker Chocolate Cake

What's in it:

- ½ C. sugar-free chocolate chips
- 1 tsp. vanilla extract
- ¾ C. unsweetened almond milk
- 4 eggs
- ½ C. melted butter
- ¼ tsp. salt
- 2 tsp. baking powder
- ¼ C. whey protein powder
- 2/3 C. cocoa powder
- ¾ C. swerve sweetener
- 1 ½ C. almond flour

How it's made:

- Grease your cooker.
- Whisk all dry recipe components together. Then stir in all wet ingredients into dry components together till combined.
- Pour batter into cooker. Set to heat on low 2 ½ - 3 hours.

- Turn cooker off and let sit 20-30 minutes. Cut into pieces and serve warm and gooey with a dollop of whipped cream.

Pumpkin Chocolate Lava Cake

What's in it:

- 2 C. milk chocolate chips
- 1 box instant chocolate pudding mix
- 2 C. cold milk
- 1 tsp. pumpkin pie spice
- 1 C. pumpkin puree
- 1/3 C. brown sugar
- 3 eggs
- 1/3 C. vegetable oil
- 1 C. water
- 1 box yellow cake mix

How it's made:

- Grease your cooker.
- Combine pie spice, brown sugar, pumpkin puree, eggs, vegetable oil, water, and cake mix together. Beat with an electric mixer for 2 minutes till very smooth. Pour into cooker.

- Mix milk and pudding mix together. Pour pudding mixture over cake batter. Then sprinkle chocolate chips in.
- Set to heat on high 2 ½ - 3 hours.
- Turn cooker off and let sit 10 minutes. Serve with whipped or ice cream and indulge!

Maple Pumpkin Spice Chex Mix

What's in it:

- 1 tbsp. vanilla extract
- 1-2 + tbsp. pumpkin pie spice
- ¼ C. light brown sugar
- ½ C. maple syrup
- ½ C. melted unsalted butter
- 1 ½ chopped graham crackers
- 1 ½ - 2 C. pretzels
- 1 ½ - 2 C. nuts of choice
- 2 C. dried fruit of choice
- 6 C. Chex cereal

How it's made:

- Add graham crackers, pretzels, dried fruit, and cereal to your cooker.
- Melt butter and then mix in pumpkin pie spice, brown sugar, maple syrup, and vanilla. Drizzle butter mixture over dry components within cooker. Stir well to coat.

- Set to heat on high 2 hours, making sure to stir every 20 minutes or so. Heat till you no longer see liquid within your cooker.

- When done, toss well and pour out onto a baking sheet for 2 hours to dry.

Pumpkin Pie Cake

What's in it:

- ½ tsp. salt
- ½ tsp. ground cloves
- ½ tsp. pumpkin pie spice
- ½ tsp. cinnamon
- 1 ½ tsp. baking soda
- 1 ½ tsp. baking powder
- 1 ½ C. all-purpose flour
- 15 ounce pure pumpkin
- 3 room temp eggs
- 2 C. brown sugar
- ½ C. softened unsalted butter

How it's made:

- With foil, line your cooker and spray with heating spray.
- Cream butter and sugar together. Then pour 1 egg in at a time, beating well after each addition. Stir in pumpkin.

- Combine salt, spices, baking soda and powder, and flour together.
- Stir in flour mixture with pumpkin mixture. Pour into cooker.
- Set to heat on high 3 hours.
- Serve with ice or whipped cream. Enjoy!

Peach Cobbler

What's in it:

- 1 tsp. cinnamon
- ½ C. brown sugar
- 2/3 C. dry quick oats
- 1/3 C. buttermilk baking mix
- ½ C. peach juice
- 4 C. sliced peaches

How it's made:

- Grease your cooker. Pour sliced peaches into the base of cooker.
- Mix cinnamon, brown sugar, oats, and baking mix together. Sprinkle this mixture over peaches. Then pour peach juice over everything and give entire mixture a light mixing.
- Set to heat on low 5 hours.
- Serve with ice cream or frozen yogurt!

Conclusion

Thank you for reading Slow Cooker Recipes.

I hope that this cookbook was able to show you that it is possible to create delicious and healthy homemade meals in a snap! Thanks to the cooker, becoming a master chef in the comfort of your own kitchen can be possible!

I hope that you did not only found recipes that caught your eye, but now have the motivation to attempt some of them yourself! Whether you are heating for yourself, family, or friends, everyone will drool over the recipes that you have skimmed through!

I hope that this book provided you with the tools you need to succeed in the kitchen and achieve your goals of living a healthier lifestyle.

The next step is to pick a recipe and start heating! You will never know which recipes from this book work the best for you or provide you with a guilty but healthy pleasure unless you make them and devour them yourself!

If you found this book valuable and useful in anyway, please take a moment to go to Amazon and leave a review! Thanks so much!

Printed in Great Britain
by Amazon